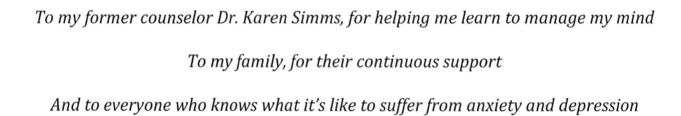

To my former counselor Dr. Karen Simms, for helping me learn to manage my mind

To my family, for their continuous support

And to everyone who knows what it's like to suffer from anxiety and depression

TABLE OF CONTENTS

Introduction

When someone says , "I'm going to eat my feelings", this usually translates to something like, "I'm going to eat an entire gallon of ice cream and cry my eyes out while I watch TV." But what if I told you that there was an intelligent and mindful way to, in a sense, "eat your feelings"?

The purpose of this book is not to promote food as a "cure-all", or to denounce modern medicine. Rather, the purpose of this book is to show you how to use food and nutrition to promote optimal mental health and optimal quality of life. Even with modern medicine, and the most advanced clinical treatments, one cannot expect to have an optimal quality of life if they have poor nutritional habits.

Anxiety and depression are becoming increasingly prevalent in our society; and mental health is an issue that has long been overlooked. My experiences with anxiety, depression, anorexia, orthorexia, vitamin B12 toxicity, iron deficiency anemia, panic attacks, and sleep paralysis inspired me to change the way I looked at food.

Instead of turning to prescription medications, I decided to eat my medicine. I discovered firsthand, the healing properties of food. This foundation of good nutrition also allowed me to discover the healing properties of exercise, meditation, and faith.

I have put together this book in the hopes that it becomes a valuable resource to those who need it.

Nutrition Philosophy

When I first began writing this book, I knew that I did not want to put another "gluten-free, dairy-free, raw vegan, sugar free, low carb, paleo" cookbook on the market. The purpose of this book is not to make you "quit" or "give up" foods that you love. The purpose of this book is not to make you feel scared or guilty. Why? Because I've experienced anorexia and orthorexia, and I know the mental exhaustion that comes with having these attitudes toward food.

Are there gluten- free, dairy free, vegetarian, and vegan recipes included in this book? Yes. Will you still find ingredients like breadcrumbs (gasp!), cheese (gasp!!), sour cream (gasp!!!), chocolate chips (gasp!!!!) and puff pastry (GASP!) in this book? Yes. This is because I believe there is a time and place for all types of food. And that includes the old family recipes made with large amounts of sugar, multiple sticks of butter, refined white flour, etc. Are these recipes "healthy"? Not by the conventional sense. However, these recipes are nostalgic. They are filled with memories. They are eaten during times of celebration with loved ones.

The intense feelings of fear and worry that are associated with eating certain foods, are more detrimental than simply eating those foods and enjoying them. Furthermore, if you allow yourself to fully enjoy these types of foods on those special occasions, then you will stay motivated to make more healthful choices through the rest of the year.

My Top Nutrition Priorities
- *Supporting organic, humanely raised meat and dairy products*
- *Supporting local farmers whenever possible*
- *Tailoring recipes to meet the preferences, needs, and goals of individuals (vegan, vegetarian, allergy-friendly, etc.)*
- *Preparing food in a way that maximizes nutrient absorption, benefit, and taste*

Optimal Food Sources
- *Organic grass fed lean beef*
- *Organic grass fed lean pork*
- *Organic grass/vegetarian fed poultry*
- *Organic milks, yogurts, cheeses (from grass fed cow, sheep, or goat)*
- *Organic free range eggs*
- *Wild caught fish*
- *Organic produce*
- *Organic nuts, seeds, legumes, and beans*
- *Organic whole grains*
- *Organic grass fed butter*
- *Organic high-quality cooking oils in glass bottles (unrefined coconut oil, extra virgin olive oil, pistachio oil, etc.)*

Ingredients I Avoid
- *Aspartame or artificial sweeteners*
- *Fat Free products/diet products/100 Calorie packs, etc.*
- *Partially or fully hydrogenated oils (aka TRANS FAT)*
- *Anything deep fried*
- *Preservatives (calcium propionate, etc.)*
- *Carrageenan*
- *Locust Bean Gum*
- *Guar Gum*
- *Egg beaters/egg substitute*

- *Anything imitation (vanilla, crab, etc.)*
- *Anything with artificial dye/food coloring (Red #40, etc.)*
- *Vegetable oil*
- *Soybean oil/Soy Products*
- *Crisco*
- *Margarine*
- *Excess alcohol*
- *Excess fruit juice*
- *Excess soda*
- *Excess refined sugar*
- *MSG*

Disclaimers

- *The % RDI's (recommended daily intake) per serving are estimates.*
- *These lists of foods are not all-inclusive. They are simply a place to start.*
- *I do not propose that these foods are a "cure-all". The information in this book is only meant to help you improve your quality of life.*
- *None of the information in this book is intended to replace a medical diagnosis. Please consult a medical professional regarding the use of prescription medications.*
- *I do not take credit for any of the images displayed in the charts in the appendices. Citations have been provided for these images on pages 189-192.*

Extra Notes

If you see this written next to a recipe:
(V)= *Vegan*
(GF)= *Gluten-Free*
(DF) = *Dairy Free*
(VT) = *Vegetarian*

Any recipe that calls for eggs can be made with flax egg or chia egg instead. For every egg used in the recipe, combine 1 T ground flaxseed or chia seed with 3 T of water and let sit in the fridge for 15 minutes.

ANXIETY

Anxiety disorders affect 40 million people in the United States age 18 and older, making them the most common mental illness in the nation (NIMH). On average, 1 in 8 children are diagnosed with an anxiety disorder each year (helpguide). Anti-anxiety prescription use has increased by 16% in the past 10 years (helpguide). Clearly, people in this country are struggling to manage their anxiety, and the multi-billion dollar pharmaceutical industry is more than willing to "help".

The Pharmacy Prescription:

Some of the most commonly prescribed anti-anxiety medications are Benzodiazepines (or Anxiolytics). They work by increasing levels of the calming neurotransmitters in the brain; which are serotonin, norepinephrine, and GABA (gamma-aminobutyric acid). Usually they begin working within 30 minutes to an hour.

However, the side effects and health risks associated with anti-anxiety medication can be just as (if not more) distressing and debilitating than anxiety itself.

Most Common Side Effects:
- Nausea
- Blurred or double vision
- Headache
- Confusion
- Tiredness
- Nightmares
- Dizziness

Less Common but *Serious* Side Effects:
- Over-sedation, appearance of drunkenness
- Drowsiness
- Slow reflexes
- Depression
- Suicidal thoughts
- Impaired thinking and judgment
- Memory loss, forgetfulness
- Emotional blunting and numbness (blocked feelings of pleasure and pain)
- Mania
- Hostility and rage
- Aggression
- Impulsive behavior

- Hallucinations
- Difficulty breathing
- Seizures
- Swelling of the face, eyes, lips, tongue, or throat
- Difficulty speaking

The Kitchen Prescription:

In terms of treating anxiety, whether its Generalized Anxiety Disorder, Panic Disorder, or Social Anxiety Disorder, the main goal is to increase levels of the calming neurotransmitters in the brain; which are serotonin, norepinephrine, and GABA (gamma-aminobutyric acid). Eating the right types of foods is one of the easiest and most effective ways to do this.

1. Increasing GABA Levels

The amino acid L-Glutamine is the precursor for GABA production in the brain. L-Glutamine, the most abundant amino acid in the body, is also one of the "non-essential amino acids". Unlike tryptophan (see pg.11), L-Glutamine passes very easily through the blood-brain-barrier. Although it is produced naturally in the body, anxiety, psychological stress, and other factors, increase the body's demand for glutamine. Without adequate dietary intake or supplementation, glutamine stores can become depleted.

> **L-Glutamine Rich Foods → Increased levels of Glutamine→ Stimulates GABA production in the brain**

L-Glutamine Rich Foods:
- Lean grass fed beef
- Lean grass fed bison
- Lean free-range chicken
- Free range eggs
- Raw yogurt
- Raw cheese
- Red cabbage (the most dense vegetable form of L-glutamine)

2. Increasing Norepinephrine Levels

The amino acid tyrosine is converted to dopamine, which is then converted to norepinephrine in the brain. As mentioned in the *Depression* section on pg. 10, increasing dopamine and norepinephrine go hand-in-hand. The amino acids phenylalanine and tyrosine are the precursors for dopamine production, while dopamine is the precursor for norepinephrine production. Omega 3 fatty acids and folate (Vitamin B9) also increase dopamine and norepinephrine.

Phenylalanine and Tyrosine → Dopamine → Norepinephrine

Phenylalanine + Tyrosine + Omega 3's + Folic Acid= Increased Dopamine and Norepinephrine Levels

---

Foods Rich in Omega 3 Fatty Acids:
- Chia Seeds (61% RDI per oz.)
- Flaxseeds (39% RDI per oz.)
- Walnuts (66% RDI per oz.)
- Wild Caught Salmon (42% RDI per serving)
- Wild Caught Mackerel (174% RDI per serving)
- Wild Caught Tuna (35% RDI per serving)
- Wild Caught Herring (47% RDI per serving)
- Lean Grass-Fed Beef (46% RDI per serving)

Foods Rich in Folate (Vitamin B9):
- Spinach (65% RDI per serving)
- Collard Greens (44% RDI per serving)
- Mustard Greens (26% RDI per serving)
- Avocado (22% RDI per serving)
- Broccoli (24% RDI per serving)
- Brussels Sprouts (25% RDI per serving)
- Beets (21% RDI per serving
- Lentils (90% RDI per serving)
- Peanuts (21% RDI per serving)
- Almonds (12% RDI per serving)
- Sunflower Seeds (22 % RDI per serving)
- Flaxseeds (14% RDI per serving)
- Papaya (29% RDI per serving)

DEPRESSION

Each year, 14.8 million Americans experience Major Depressive Disorder (Facts). One in 10 Americans take an anti-depressant (Rabin). One in four American women in their 40's/50's take an anti-depressant (Rabin). In other words, people are desperately searching for a way to feel better, and the multi-billion dollar pharmaceutical industry is more than happy to "help".

The Pharmacy Prescription:

The most commonly prescribed antidepressants are classified as either SSRIs (Selective Serotonin Reuptake Inhibitors) or SSNRIs (Selective Serotonin and Norepinephrine Reuptake Inhibitors).

Serotonin and norepinephrine are feel-good neurotransmitters produced in the brain. These medications work by preventing the re-uptake of serotonin and/or norepinephrine. This keeps the levels of serotonin and/or norepinephrine in the brain higher, helping to improve your mood.

However, the side effects and health risks associated with antidepressants can be just as (if not more) distressing and debilitating than depression itself.

Most Common Side Effects:
- Nausea
- Weight gain/increased appetite
- Loss of libido and erectile problems
- Fatigue and drowsiness
- Insomnia
- Dry mouth
- Blurred vision
- Constipation
- Dizziness
- Agitation
- Anxiety
- Irritability

Less Common but *Serious* Side Effects:
- Suicidal thoughts
- Diabetes
- Serotonin Syndrome
- Psychosis

The Kitchen Prescription:

In terms of treating depression, the main goal is to increase levels of feel-good neurotransmitters in the brain. The main feel-good neurotransmitters are serotonin, dopamine, norepinephrine, and endorphins.

Most people don't start to experience the full positive effects of antidepressant medication until 6 to 8 weeks after they start taking it (psychcentral). But, eating the right foods can help you feel better—not within weeks—but *minutes.*

1. Increasing Serotonin Levels

The amino acid tryptophan is the precursor for serotonin production. Since tryptophan is an amino acid, it is found primarily in protein rich foods. So, in theory, eating protein rich foods should help increase your serotonin levels. It turns out though, that this is only one part of the equation. To increase serotonin levels in the brain, tryptophan has to pass through the blood-brain-barrier. This is a difficult task, because tryptophan must compete with all the amino acids at the blood-brain-barrier transport site. The only way for tryptophan to pass through the blood-brain-barrier is with the help of carbohydrates. This is because carbohydrate consumption leads to insulin production; and insulin suppresses levels of all the amino acids---*except* for tryptophan.

> **Tryptophan Rich Foods + Low-Glycemic Carbohydrates = Increased Serotonin Levels**

Amino Acid Rich Foods (Tryptophan, Phenylalanine, Tyrosine, etc.):
- Pumpkin Seeds (58% RDI per oz.)
- Chia seeds (44% RDI per oz.)
- Sesame Seeds (39% RDI per oz.)
- Sunflower seeds (35% RDI per oz.)
- Flaxseeds (30% RDI per oz.)
- Cashews (24% RDI per oz.)
- Pistachios (29% RDI per oz.)
- Almonds (21% RDI per oz.)
- Hazelnuts (19% RDI per oz.)
- Mozzarella Cheese (57% RDI per oz.)
- Plain Greek Yogurt (22% RDI per serving)
- Cow's Milk (16% RDI per serving)
- Plain Yogurt (18% RDI per serving)

- Parmesan Cheese (56% RDI per oz.)
- Goat Cheese (17% RDI per oz.)
- Pork Tenderloin (117% RDI per serving)
- Lean Grass-Fed Beef (121% RDI per serving)
- Lean Chicken and Turkey (white or dark meat-123% RDI per serving)
- Wild Caught Halibut (102% RDI per serving)
- Wild Caught Salmon (98% RDI per serving)
- Wild Caught Cod (70% RDI per serving)
- Wild Caught Snapper (89% RDI per serving)
- Wild Caught Mackerel (88% RDI per serving)
- Wild Caught Haddock (79% RDI per serving)
- Wild Caught Tuna (34% RDI per serving)
- Wild Caught Shrimp (79% RDI per serving)
- Wild Caught Lobster (75% RDI per serving)
- Wild Caught Clams (87% RDI per serving)
- Wild Caught Scallops (53% RDI per serving)
- Whole Oats (130% per serving)
- Buckwheat (116% per serving)
- Wheat Bran (59% per serving)
- Eggs (30% RDI per egg)
- Beans and Lentils (60% RDI per serving)

Low Glycemic Carbohydrate Foods:
- Eggplant
- Carrots
- Summer Squash
- Zucchini
- Butternut Squash
- Jicama
- Pumpkin
- Sweet Potatoes
- Bell Peppers
- Green Beans
- Broccoli
- Apples
- Plums
- Oranges
- Lemons
- Cranberries

- Grapefruit
- Blackberries
- Raspberries
- Blueberries
- Strawberries
- Beans and Lentils
- Plain Yogurt
- Barley
- Buckwheat
- Oats
- Quinoa
- Rye
- 100% Whole Grain Bread

Notes:

For more information of Glycemic Index and Glycemic Load, see the "Glycemic Load" and "Glycemic Index" charts on pages 175 and 176.

For more Low-Glycemic carbohydrate sources see the "Guide to Grains" chart on pg. 165

2. Increasing Dopamine and Norepinephrine Levels

Increasing dopamine and norepinephrine go hand-in-hand. The amino acids phenylalanine and tyrosine are the precursors for dopamine production, while dopamine is the precursor for norepinephrine production. Omega 3 fatty acids and Folate (Vitamin B9) also increase dopamine and norepinephrine.

Phenylalanine and Tyrosine → Dopamine → Norepinephrine

Phenylalanine + Tyrosine + Omega 3's + Folic Acid= Increased Dopamine and Norepinephrine Levels

Foods Rich in Omega 3 Fatty Acids:
- Chia Seeds (61% RDI per serving)
- Flaxseeds (39% RDI per serving)
- Walnuts (66% RDI per serving)
- Wild Caught Salmon (42% RDI per serving)
- Wild Caught Mackerel (174% RDI per serving)
- Wild Caught Tuna (35% RDI per serving)
- Wild Caught Herring (47% RDI per serving)
- Lean Grass-Fed Beef (46% RDI per serving)

Foods Rich in Folate (vitamin B9):
- Spinach (65% RDI per serving)
- Collard Greens (44% RDI per serving)
- Mustard Greens (26% RDI per serving)
- Avocado (22% RDI per serving)
- Broccoli (24% RDI per serving)
- Brussels Sprouts (25% RDI per serving)
- Beets (21% RDI per serving)
- Lentils (90% RDI per serving)
- Peanuts (21% RDI per serving)
- Almonds (12% RDI per serving)
- Sunflower Seeds (22 % RDI per serving)
- Flaxseeds (14% RDI per serving)
- Papaya (29% RDI per serving)

3. Increasing Endorphin Levels

Endorphins are neurotransmitters in the brain that act as the body's natural painkillers. They are released in response to situations that the brain perceives as "painful", such as exercise. This is what creates the so-called "runner's high". Research has shown that people with depression, chronic fatigue syndrome, and fibromyalgia have low levels of endorphins. Vitamin C stimulates endorphin production, as do the N-acylethanolamine group of chemicals found in dark chocolate. Similarly, capsaicin, the compound in spicy foods, stimulates the release of endorphins. This is because the brain interprets the burning sensation on the tongue as "painful".

Vitamin C and/or N-acylethanolamine→ Stimulates endorphin production in the brain

Capsaicin→ "Pain" response→ Brain releases endorphins

Foods Rich in Capsaicin:
- Jalapeño Peppers
- Habanero Peppers
- Chili Peppers
- Cayenne Pepper
- Serrano Peppers
- Red Chili Flakes

Foods Rich in Vitamin C:
- Papaya (224% RDI per serving)
- Bell Peppers (157% RDI per serving)
- Broccoli (135% RDI per serving)
- Brussels Sprouts (129% RDI per serving)
- Strawberries (113% RDI per serving)
- Pineapple (105% RDI per serving)
- Oranges (93% RDI per serving)
- Lemon (31% RDI per serving)
- Lime (31% RDI per serving)
- Grapefruit (59% RDI per serving)
- Kiwifruit (85% RDI per serving)
- Cantaloupe (78% RDI per serving)
- Cauliflower (73% RDI per serving)
- Tomatoes (33% RDI per serving)

- *Dark Chocolate (at least 60% dark): **N-acylethanolamine chemicals**

ANXIETY AND DEPRESSION: THE CONNECTION

Depression and anxiety disorders are often lumped together under the umbrella category of "mental health conditions"; and they are deeply connected to the brain. However, anyone who has experienced feelings of anxiety and/or depression knows that mood isn't the only thing that is affected.

Other Ways Depression Can Affect Us:
- Poor concentration
- Insomnia
- Apathy
- Fatigue
- Digestive problems
- Weight gain (often due to emotional eating)
- Weight loss (often due to lack of appetite)
- Social isolation

Other Ways Anxiety Can Affect Us:
- Poor concentration
- Insomnia
- Fatigue
- Restlessness
- Weight gain (often due to emotional eating)
- Weight loss (often due to lack of appetite)
- Abnormal heart rhythms
- Excessive sweating
- Digestive problems

Serotonin, dopamine, GABA, norepinephrine, and endorphins are big players when it comes to addressing overall mood, mental concentration, heart rhythms, etc...

But what about: INSOMNIA, FATIGUE, EMOTIONAL EATING, and DIGESTIVE PROBLEMS?

Keep Reading!

INSOMNIA

Insomnia is a very common problem, with over 3 million cases diagnosed each year in the United States (Romm). But, according to a 2007 study from the NIH, on average, prescription sleeping pills will only add about 11 minutes of additional sleep time (Sleeping).

The Pharmacy Prescription:

The most common types of sleeping pills are *Diphenhydramine*-based over-the-counter medications, *selective GABA* medications, and *sleep-wake cycle modifiers.* *Diphenhydramine*- based medications are antihistamines that are used to treat allergic reactions and symptoms of the common cold. They are also used to promote sleep. *Selective GABA* medications target specific types of GABA receptors in the brain that are responsible for our level of alertness and relaxation. *Sleep-wake cycle modifiers* work by binding to melatonin receptors in the area of the brain that controls the body's circadian rhythm (aka, sleep-wake cycle), which promotes relaxation and sleepiness.

However, all types of sleeping pills can cause a variety of side effects.

Most Common Side Effects of *Diphenhydramine*-Based Medications:
- Drowsiness
- Dizziness
- Constipation
- Upset stomach
- Blurred vision
- Dry mouth

Less Common But *Serious* Side Effects of *Diphenhydramine*-Based Medications:
- Mood changes
- Restlessness
- Delirium
- Difficulty urinating
- Fast/irregular heartbeat
- Seizures
- Rash
- Itching/swelling of the face, tongue, throat
- Severe dizziness
- Trouble breathing

Most Common Side Effects of *Selective GABA* Medications:
- Drowsiness
- Infection
- Change in taste
- Nausea
- Dizziness
- Dry-mouth

Less Common But *Serious* Side Effects of *Selective GABA* Medications:
- Fever
- Bladder pain
- Anxiety
- Depression
- Nervousness
- Lack of appetite
- Nerve pain
- Hallucinations
- Poor concentration
- Nerve pain

Most Common Side Effects of *Sleep-Wake-Cycle Modifier* Medications:
- Dizziness
- Drowsiness
- Fatigue
- Body aches or pain
- Change in taste
- Muscle aches or cramps

Less Common But *Serious* Side Effects of *Sleep-Wake-Cycle Modifier* Medications:
- Difficulty breathing
- Difficulty moving
- Depression
- Swollen joints
- Poor concentration
- Fever
- Vomiting

The Kitchen Prescription:

In terms of treating insomnia, the main goal is to increase levels of melatonin, and decrease levels of adrenaline and cortisol before bedtime. Melatonin is a hormone made in the pineal grand of the brain that helps control the sleep-wake cycle. Higher levels of melatonin prepare the body for sleep, while lower levels of melatonin prepare the body for staying awake. Adrenaline (or epinephrine) is a hormone produced by the adrenal glands during the fight or flight response. Increased levels of adrenaline cause increased respiration, increased heart rate, and increased alertness. Cortisol is known as the "stress hormone". It is produced by the adrenal glands during the fight or flight response. It influences blood sugar levels, metabolism, immune function, blood pressure, blood vessel contraction, and the inflammatory response. Both high levels of cortisol (from chronic stress), and low levels of cortisol (from adrenal fatigue), can contribute to insomnia.

1. Increase melatonin levels

Serotonin is the precursor to melatonin. Serotonin and melatonin also have the same amino acid precursor, L-tryptophan. Hence, the foods listed on pg. 11 and 12 that increase serotonin production can also be used to increase melatonin production.

2. Decrease adrenaline and cortisol levels

Magnesium is an important electrolyte that deactivates adrenaline and reduces cortisol, which promotes optimal sleep. It also has muscle-relaxing properties and helps reduce muscle cramps. It is important to note that adequate levels of vitamin D3, vitamin B1 (thiamine), vitamin B6 (pyridoxine), vitamin E, and selenium promote optimal absorption of magnesium.

Tryptophan rich foods + Low Glycemic Carbohydrates = Increased Melatonin Levels (see pg. 12 and 13)

Magnesium rich foods + Vitamin D3 rich foods + Vitamin B1 rich foods + Vitamin B6 rich foods + Vitamin E rich foods + Selenium rich foods = Decreased Adrenaline and Cortisol Levels

---

Foods Rich in Magnesium:
- Spinach (39% RDI per serving)
- Swiss Chard (38% RDI per serving)
- Kale (19% RDI per serving)
- Collard Greens (13% RDI per serving)
- Turnip Greens (11% RDI per serving)
- Pumpkin Seeds (37% RDI per serving)
- Sesame Seeds (63% RDI per serving)
- Brazil Nuts (63% RDI per serving)
- Almonds (48% RDI per serving)
- Cashews (44% RDI per serving)
- Pine Nuts (43% RDI per serving)
- Peanuts (31% RDI per serving)
- Pecans (17% RDI per serving)
- Walnuts (16 RDI per serving)
- Mackerel (24% RDI per serving)
- Chickpeas (20 % RDI per serving)
- White Beans (28 RDI per serving)
- Brown Rice (21% RDI per serving)
- Quinoa (30% RDI per serving)
- Millet (19% RDI per serving)
- Buckwheat (13% RDI per serving)
- Avocado (10% RDI per serving)
- Plain Yogurt (12% RDI per serving)
- Cow's Milk (10% RDI per serving)
- Banana (10% RDI per serving)
- Dried Figs (13% RDI per serving)
- Dark Chocolate (24% RDI per serving)
- Molasses (12% RDI per serving)

Foods Rich in Vitamin D3:
- Cod Liver Oil (83% RDI per serving)
- Wild Caught Trout (108% RDI per serving)
- Wild Caught Salmon (97% RDI per serving)
- Wild Caught Swordfish (94% RDI per serving)
- Wild Caught Halibut (33% RDI per serving)
- Portobello Mushrooms (63% RDI per serving)
- Maitake Mushrooms (131% RDI per serving)
- Morel Mushrooms (23% RDI per serving)

- Chanterelle Mushrooms (19% RDI per serving)
  *(Mushrooms exposed to sunlight when growing or before eating contain more vitamin D)
- Buttermilk (21% RDI per serving)
- Fortified Cow's Milk (20% RDI per serving)
- Goat's Milk (21% RDI per serving)
- Egg Yolk (20% RDI per serving)

Foods Rich in Vitamin B1 (Thiamine):
- Wild Caught Trout (18% RDI per serving)
- Wild Caught Salmon (19% RDI per serving)
- Pork Tenderloin (57% RDI per serving)
- Pork Chops, Bone-in (51% RDI per serving)
- Sunflower Seeds (28% RDI per serving)
- Flax Seeds (31% RDI per serving)
- Sesame Seeds (22% RDI per serving)
- Chia Seeds (16% RDI per serving)
- Macadamia Nuts (13% RDI per serving)
- Pistachios (13% RDI per serving)
- Brazil Nuts (12% RDI per serving)
- Green Peas (28% RDI per serving)
- Navy Beans (36% RDI per serving)
- Black Beans (35% RDI per serving)
- Barley (33% RDI per serving)
- Lentils (28% RDI per serving)
- Pinto Beans (28% RDI per serving)
- Lima Beas (25% RDI per serving)
- Oats (25% RDI per serving)

Foods Rich in Vitamin B6 (Pyridoxine):
- Sunflower Seeds (19% RDI per serving)
- Sesame Seeds (11% RDI per serving)
- Pistachios (16% RDI per serving)
- Wild Caught Tuna (44% RDI per serving)
- Wild Caught Salmon (40% RDI per serving)
- Wild Caught Halibut (27% RDI per serving)
- Wild Caught Swordfish (26% RDI per serving)
- Wild Caught Herring (22% RDI per serving)
- Turkey Breast (46% RDI per serving)

- Boneless, Skinless Chicken Breast (28% RDI per serving)
- Pork Tenderloin (36% RDI per serving)
- Pork Chops (30% RDI per serving)
- Lean Grass-Fed Beef (44% RDI per serving)
- Sweet Potato (36% RDI per serving)
- Potatoes (32% RDI per serving)
- Spinach (26% RDI per serving)
- Banana (25% RDI per serving)
- Prunes (20% RDI per serving)
- Dried Apricots (16% RDI per serving)

Foods Rich in Vitamin E:
- Sunflower Seeds (82% RDI per serving)
- Almonds (40% RDI per serving)
- Spinach (25% RDI per serving)
- Swiss Chard (22% RDI per serving)
- Avocado (21% RDI per serving)
- Peanuts (20% RDI per serving)
- Hazelnuts (20% RDI per serving)
- Turnip Greens (18% RDI per serving)
- Beet Greens (17% RDI per serving)
- Papaya (17% RDI per serving)
- Mustard Greens (17% RDI per serving)
- Olives (20% RDI per serving)

Note*: Vitamins A, E, D, and K are the 4 fat-soluble vitamins. So, for optimal absorption they should be cooked or eaten with healthy fats. For more information on healthy fats, see the "Introduction" section on pg.4*

Foods Rich in Selenium:
- Brazil Nuts (767% RDI per serving)
- Sunflower Seeds (32% RDI per serving)
- Chia Seeds (22% RDI per serving)
- Sesame Seeds (14% RDI per serving)
- Flax Seeds (10% RDI per serving)
- Wild Caught Oysters (187% RDI per serving)
- Wild Caught Lobster (89% RDI per serving)
- Wild Caught Clams (78% RDI per serving)
- Wild Caught Shrimp (60% RDI per serving)

- Wild Caught Tuna (131% RDI per serving)
- Wild Caught Swordfish (83% RDI per serving)
- Wild Caught Halibut (67% RDI per serving)
- Wild Caught Mackerel (63% RDI per serving)
- Wild Caught Snapper (60% RDI per serving)
- Lean Grass Fed Beef (48% RDI per serving)
- Turkey Breast (46% RDI per serving)
- Boneless, Skinless Chicken Breast (39% RDI per serving)
- Portobello Mushrooms (38% RDI per serving)
- White Mushrooms (21% RDI per serving)
- Rye Berries/Kernels (17% RDI per serving)
- Brown Rice (27% RDI per serving)
- Pearl Barley (18% RDI per serving)
- Oats (18% RDI Per serving)

Foods Rich in Melatonin:
- Tart cherries and grapes are the only two fruits known to contain melatonin

Notes:
Dried tart cherries do not contain melatonin, but whole tart cherries and tart cherry juice do contain melatonin

Red and purple grapes, such as Nebbiolo, Croatina, and Merlot varieties contain the highest amounts of melatonin

FATIGUE

Over one million Americans have Chronic Fatigue Syndrome (Chronic). On top of that, it has been estimated that up to 20% of fatal road accidents are caused by driver fatigue (Fatigue). Clearly, the effects of fatigue are widespread, influencing everything from daily productivity, to life-threatening situations.

The Pharmacy Prescription:

Chronic Fatigue Syndrome is not typically treated with prescription medication. However, many people do not realize that feelings of chronic fatigue can stem from simple nutrient deficiencies.

The Kitchen Prescription:

In terms of treating fatigue, the main goal is to maintain optimal levels of iron, zinc, and vitamin B12. All of these nutrients play important roles in keeping us energized. Iron is an essential mineral. It is also a component of hemoglobin, which is the substance in red blood cells that transports oxygen throughout the body. A lack of iron → a lack of red blood cells→ a lack of oxygen transportation→ fatigue. Zinc is an essential mineral. It helps the body break down carbohydrates and proteins from food into usable sources of energy. As such, zinc deficiency can contribute to low energy levels. Like Zinc, vitamin B12 helps the body break down nutrients from food into usable sources of energy. It also promotes red blood cell production, which increases oxygen transportation and reduces fatigue.

1. Increasing Iron Levels

There are two types of iron found in food sources, heme and non-heme. Heme iron is found in animal-based foods such as red meat, poultry, and fish. It is readily absorbed in the body. Non-heme iron is found in plant-based foods such as beans, egg yolks, and seeds. It is not readily absorbed in the body without vitamin C. Consuming vitamin C rich foods along with non-heme iron helps increase absorption.

Non-Heme Iron + Vitamin C Rich Foods= Increased Iron Levels

Increased Iron Levels →Increased Oxygen Transportation→ More Energy

---

2. Increasing Zinc Levels

It is important to note that many plant-based foods that are high in zinc are also high in phytates and fiber, both of which decrease zinc absorption. Soaking beans, seeds, and grains in water for a few hours before cooking them helps decrease the level of phytates, which allows you to absorb more of the zinc that these foods contain.

> **Zinc Rich Foods + Soaking Method = Increased Zinc Levels**
>
> **Increased Zinc Levels → Stimulates Food Breakdown → More Energy**

3. Increasing Vitamin B12 Levels

It is important to note that vitamin B12 is found only in animal-based foods. This form of vitamin B12 is easily absorbed in the body. The plant-based foods that contain vitamin B12 have been fortified. This form of vitamin B12 is not easily absorbed in the body.

> **Vitamin B12 Rich Foods = Increased Vitamin B12 Levels**
>
> **Increased Vitamin B12 Levels → Stimulates Red Blood Cell Formation → Increases Oxygen Transportation → More Energy**

Foods Rich in Iron:
- Pumpkin Seeds (23% RDI per serving)
- Sesame Seeds (23% RDI per serving)
- Chia Seeds (12% RDI per serving)
- Chicken Liver (20% RDI per serving)
- Lean Beef (12% RDI per serving)
- Lentils (37% RDI per serving)
- Kidney Beans (29% RDI per serving)
- Chickpeas (26% RDI per serving)
- Black Beans (20% RDI per serving)
- Oatmeal (12% RDI per serving)
- Bulgur (10% RDI per serving)
- Swiss Chard (22% RDI per serving)
- Spinach (36% RDI per serving)

- Dark Chocolate (28% RDI per serving)
- Dried Apricots (21% RDI per serving)
- Raisins (21% RDI per serving)
- Dried Figs (17% RDI per serving)
- Prunes (26% RDI per serving)
- Molasses (4% RDI per serving)

Foods Rich in Vitamin C: (see pg. 15)
- Papaya (224% RDI per serving)
- Bell Peppers (157% RDI per serving)
- Broccoli (135% RDI per serving)
- Brussels Sprouts (129% RDI per serving)
- Strawberries (113% RDI per serving)
- Pineapple (105% RDI per serving)
- Oranges (93% RDI per serving)
- Lemon (31% RDI per serving)
- Lime (31% RDI per serving)
- Grapefruit (59% RDI per serving)
- Kiwifruit (85% RDI per serving)
- Cantaloupe (78% RDI per serving)
- Cauliflower (73% RDI per serving)
- Tomatoes (33% RDI per serving)

Foods Rich in Zinc:
- Oysters (220% RDI per serving)
- Crab (43% RDI per serving)
- Lean Beef (95% RDI per serving)
- Chicken- dark meat (15% RDI per serving)
- Pork Loin (28% RDI per serving)
- Lamb Shoulder (46% RDI per serving)
- Wheat Germ (31% RDI per serving)
- Pumpkin Seeds (19% RDI per serving)
- Sesame Seeds (19% RDI per serving)
- Sunflower Seeds (10% RDI per serving)
- Cashews (10% RDI per serving)
- Pine Nuts (12% RDI per serving)
- Adzuki Beans (27% RDI per serving)

Foods Rich in Vitamin B12:
- Wild Caught Salmon (257% RDI per serving)
- Wild Caught Mackerel (279% RDI per serving)
- Wild Caught Sardines (126% RDI per serving)
- Wild Caught Trout (106% RDI per serving)
- Wild Caught Herring (186% RDI per serving)
- Wild Caught Tuna (154% RDI per serving)
- Lean Beef (34% RDI per serving)
- Cow's Milk (82% RDI per serving)
- Plain Yogurt (15% RDI per serving)
- Swiss Cheese (60% RDI per serving)
- Eggs (6% RDI per serving)

DIGESTIVE PROBLEMS, GUT HEALTH AND EMOTIONAL EATING

As Hippocrates noted some 2500 years ago, "All disease begins in the gut". Whether its IBS, colitis, food allergies, acid reflux, heartburn, leaky gut syndrome, constipation, or diarrhea, its clear that our digestion and emotions are linked.

We've all experienced this, whether it's traveling, preparing for a presentation at work, or sleeping through your alarm. Any time we're in a state of stress and/or our "fight or flight" response kicks in, we:

- Reach for the Tums (heart burn)
- Run to the bathroom (diarrhea)
- Grab some ex-lax/suppositories (constipation)
- Start burping (acid reflux)
- Bend over with stomach cramps

Constipation occurs when peristalsis (the muscle contraction in your small intestine) happens too slowly, which causes too much water to be absorbed, and results in dry, hard stools. Often, when we process our emotions too slowly, we become lazy, indecisive, unproductive, or overwhelmed. Hence, we become constipated. Think about those times when you're traveling as an example: sitting on an airplane or in a car for many hours without moving, eating at irregular intervals, etc.

Diarrhea occurs when peristalsis happens too quickly and not enough water is absorbed, which results in watery, loose stools. Often, when we process our emotions too quickly, we become nervous, fidgety, or impulsive. Hence, we get diarrhea. Think about those times when you're about to give a presentation or heading to the starting line of a race: your mind is running at a million miles an hour, your heart is pounding and you start to sweat.

Our guts (intestines) and our brains originate from the same material. The gut responds to neurotransmitters like serotonin and adrenaline that are sent out by the brain. In fact, it is estimated that the digestive tract produces up to 90% of the body's serotonin (Microbes). This is one of the many reasons why anxiety and depression are influenced by gut health. On top of this, impaired gut health has also been linked to obesity, eating disorders, food cravings, and decreased insulin sensitivity.

Note:
See the "Food Cravings" chart on pg.157 for more information

The Kitchen Prescription for Gut Health:

Probiotic supplements are very beneficial and effective. But there are also foods you can incorporate into your diet to improve your gut health.

Foods Rich in Probiotics:
- Yogurt (with live and active cultures)
- Kefir
- Kombucha
- Miso
- Sauerkraut
- Sourdough Bread (made with live and active cultures)
- Pickled Vegetables
- Fermented Vegetables
- Traditional Cultured Buttermilk

Foods Rich in Prebiotics:
- Jicama
- Dandelion Greens
- Garlic
- Onions
- Leeks
- Wheat Germ
- Whole Wheat Berries
- Sprouted Grain Breads
- Avocado
- Apple Cider Vinegar (with "The Mother" written on the label)
- Bananas
- Asparagus
- Artichokes

Other Foods For Gut Health:
- Bone Broth
  Contains amino acid such as glutamine and glycine that help maintain the structure of the intestinal wall, promote stomach acid production, and promote bile acid production. All of these things help promote optimal digestion.
- Ginger
  Helps stimulate saliva, bile, and stomach acid production, promoting digestion. Also contains anti-inflammatory compounds that help relieve nausea

- <u>Lemon Juice</u>
  Stimulates the production of stomach acid, which helps to relieve acid reflux
- <u>Pineapple</u>
  Contains an enzyme called bromelain that helps the body digest proteins and break them down into amino acids

Note: If you have a hard time digesting raw fruits and vegetables, try steaming, stewing, or roasting them instead. Cooking fruits and vegetables makes it easier for our bodies to digest and absorb the nutrients.

Digestive Problems → Linked to Impaired Gut Health → Linked to Gut Bacteria → Linked to Serotonin Production → Influences Emotional State → Influences Emotional Eating

Emotional Eating → Linked to Food Cravings → Linked to Overeating/Eating Disorders/Binge Eating

---

PROBIOTICS	PREBIOTICS
Live, active, bacterial cultures Found in certain foods or in probiotic supplements	A form of fiber that "feeds" probiotic bacteria in the digestive tract Found in certain foods

ANXIETY FIGHTING RECIPES

The following recipes incorporate the foods listed in the "Anxiety" section (see pg. 7) into delicious, nourishing recipes that will help you overcome anxiety—without the nasty side effects from prescription medication.

Tasty Bites

1. Spice Roasted Sweet Potatoes with Tangy Yogurt Dipping Sauce **(VT) (GF)**
2. Beetroot, Cheddar, and Apple Mini Tarts **(VT)**
3. Grilled Brussels Sprouts with Aioli Dipping Sauce **(VT) (GF) (DF)**
4. Crispy Baked Broccoli "Tots" **(VT)**

Something Savory

1. Crustless Quiche with Canadian Bacon, Spinach, and Butternut Squash **(GF) (VT)**
2. Ultimate Beetroot Burger with Avocado Sauce **(VT)**
3. Halibut Fish Tacos with Cabbage and Jicama Slaw
4. Warm Lentil Salad with Toasted Walnuts and Goat Cheese **(GF)**

Something Fresh

1. Grilled Chicken Salad with Creamy Lime Dressing **(GF)**
2. Omega Power Salad with Salmon, Spinach, and Avocado **(GF) (DF)**
3. Roasted Garlic and Brown Butter Lentil Soup **(VT) (GF) (DF)**
4. Crispy Grilled Cabbage Wedges with Spicy Lime Dressing **(VT) (GF) (DF)**

Mid-Day Munchies

1. Rosemary Roasted Almonds **(V) (VT) (GF) (DF)**
2. Cocoa Spinach Smoothie **(V) (VT) (GF)**
3. Cinnamon Sunflower Seed Butter **(V) (VT) (GF) (DF)**
4. Drop Biscuits with Spinach and Cheddar **(VT)**

Something Sweet

1. Cranberry and Orange Pumpkin Seed Muffins **(GF) (VT) (DF)**
2. Soaked Buckwheat Pancakes **(VT) (GF)**
3. Six-Ingredient Flourless Peanut Butter Brownies **(VT) (GF) (DF)**
4. Simple Almond Cake **(VT) (GF) (DF)**

TASTY BITES

SPICE ROASTED SWEET POTATOES WITH TANGY YOGURT DIPPING SAUCE
Serves 4

INGREDIENTS
<u>For the Sweet Potatoes</u>
- 2 large, orange sweet potatoes
- 3 T extra virgin olive oil
- 1 t sea salt, plus more to taste
- 2 t chili powder, plus more to taste
- 1 t paprika, plus more to taste
- 1 t ground cinnamon, plus more to taste

<u>For the Yogurt Dipping Sauce</u>
- 1 C plain Greek yogurt (preferably 2% or full-fat)
- ½ lemon, juiced
- 2 T pure maple syrup

DIRECTIONS
Preheat the oven to 425°F. Cut the sweet potatoes in chunks or wedges (leaving the skin on), about ½ inch thick. Place the sweet potatoes into a large pot, fill with water, and bring to a boil. Reduce the heat to a simmer, and cook until the sweet potatoes are barely fork tender. Drain and cool.

Place the cooled sweet potatoes onto a baking sheet. Drizzle with olive oil, and sprinkle with seasonings. Toss to coat. Roast for about 20 minutes, flipping with a spatula half way through, until browned.

While the potatoes are roasting, prepare the yogurt dipping sauce. Place the Greek yogurt in a bowl, and squeeze in the lemon juice. Fold in the maple syrup and stir to combine. Taste and adjust as necessary.

BEETROOT, CHEDDAR, AND APPLE MINI TARTS
Serves 6

INGREDIENTS

- 1 sheet frozen puff pastry, thawed
- ½ C white cheddar cheese, grated
- 1 apple, finely chopped
- 1 red beetroot, blanched, peeled, and finely chopped
- 2-3 T honey
- 1 t ground cinnamon
- 1 t fresh lemon juice
- Sea salt, to taste
- 1 T extra virgin olive oil

DIRECTIONS

Preheat the oven to 400°F. Cut rounds from the puff pastry sheet, using a 4-inch round cutter. Place the pastry rounds on a parchment lined baking sheet, and prick each round all over with a fork.

Heat olive oil in a pan over medium- high heat. Add the beetroot and apple, and cook until softened. Add cinnamon, sea salt, and stir. Spoon the mixture onto each pastry round, leaving room around the edges. Top each round with a sprinkle of grated cheddar, and bake for 10-15 minutes until the pastry is golden.

Combine the honey and lemon juice in a small bowl and drizzle over the cooked tarts. Serve warm or at room temperature.

Note: Often times, store bought frozen puff pastry is filled with trans fat, artificial flavors, and other nasty ingredients. See pg. 182 for a list of good quality store bought brands. If you want to make your own puff pastry from scratch, see pg.184-189 for a traditional recipe, vegan recipe, and gluten free recipe.

GRILLED BRUSSELS SPROUTS WITH AIOLI DIPPING SAUCE

Serves 6-8

INGREDIENTS

For the Brussels Sprouts
- 20 brussels sprouts, cut in half lengthwise
- Extra virgin olive oil
- Sea salt and black pepper

For the Aioli Dipping Sauce
- ½ C mayonnaise
- 1 t grainy Dijon mustard
- ½ t minced garlic
- 1 t fresh lemon juice
- 1 t paprika

DIRECTIONS

Place brussels sprouts onto a large sheet of aluminum foil. Drizzle with olive oil, sprinkle with sea salt and pepper, and toss to coat. Bring the ends of the aluminum foil together, wrap, and seal the ends.

Heat the grill to 400°F. Place the foil packet on the grill for 15-20 minutes, until the brussels sprouts are fork tender and golden brown.

Combine the mayonnaise, mustard, garlic, lemon juice, and paprika in a bowl. Place the brussels sprouts on a platter next to the bowl of dipping sauce. Serve warm or at room temperature.

CRISPY BAKED BROCCOLI "TOTS"
Serves 6

INGREDIENTS
- 2 C broccoli florets
- 1 or 2 large eggs, depending on desired consistency
- ¼ C diced sweet onion
- 1/4 C cheddar cheese, grated
- 2/3 C panko breadcrumbs, plus 2 T
- Sea salt, to taste
- Paprika, to taste
- Garlic powder, to taste
- Black pepper, to taste

DIRECTIONS
Preheat the oven to 400°F. Grease a baking sheet with a thin layer of olive oil, or line with parchment paper.

Cut the broccoli florets into large chunks and pulse in a food processor until very finely chopped. Transfer to a large bowl and combine with egg, onion, cheddar, breadcrumbs, and seasonings.

Place about 2 T of the mixture into your hands, and form into a tater tot shape. Place each tot on the baking sheet. Once all the tots have been formed, take the additional 2 T of breadcrumbs, and sprinkle over the top of each tot, gently pressing into the surface.

Bake for about 25 minutes, until golden brown and crisp. Serve hot with your favorite dipping sauce (ketchup, mustard, ranch, etc.)

SOMETHING SAVORY

CRUSTLESS QUICHE WITH CANADIAN BACON, SPINACH, AND BUTTERNUT SQUASH

Serves 4-6

INGREDIENTS

- 8 slices of uncured Canadian bacon, roughly chopped
- 2 C baby spinach
- ½ of a small butternut squash, deseeded and cut into ¼ inch disks
- 6 eggs
- Extra virgin olive oil
- ½ C sour cream (optional)
- 1 t sea salt
- 1 t black pepper
- ¼ t garlic powder

DIRECTIONS

Preheat oven to 375°F. Coat the sides and bottom of a pie dish or tart pan with a thin layer of olive oil. Line with parchment paper if desired. In a medium bowl, whisk together the eggs, sour cream (if using), and seasonings. Heat a small amount of oil in a skillet over medium high heat. Add the spinach, and sauté.

Line the bottom of the dish with one layer of butternut squash disks. Sprinkle half of the chopped Canadian bacon on top. Lay the sautéed spinach on top of the squash and Canadian bacon.

Put another layer of butternut squash disks over the spinach, and sprinkle with the remaining Canadian bacon. Pour the egg mixture evenly over the top. Bake for about 45 minutes, until golden brown and cooked through.

ULTIMATE BEETROOT BURGER
WITH AVOCADO SAUCE
Serves 4-6

INGREDIENTS
<u>For the Burgers</u>
- 2 C red beetroot, peeled and cut into large chunks
- 1 C red or white quinoa, cooked (see pg. 165 for cooking instructions, remembering to rinse dry quinoa before cooking)
- 1 T extra virgin olive oil
- ¼ sweet onion, diced
- 1 garlic clove, minced
- 2 large eggs
- ½ C panko breadcrumbs
- 1 ½ t sea salt
- Seeded, whole wheat buns (or a loaf of seeded, whole wheat bread that can be cut into a top and bottom bun)

<u>For the Avocado Sauce</u>
- 1 large ripe avocado
- 2 T plain Greek yogurt or sour cream
- 3 T fresh lime juice
- 1 ½ t chili powder

DIRECTIONS
Preheat the oven to 375°F. Place the beetroot onto a foil-lined baking dish and roast for 30 minutes, until fork tender. Remove from the oven and set aside to cool. Place the beets into a food processor, and lightly pulse. Leave a good amount of texture and avoid completely mashing the beets.

Transfer the beets into a large bowl and add all ingredients and combine. If the texture is too mushy, gradually add more breadcrumbs until the desired consistency is reached. Shape the burgers into patties and place on an uncovered plate in the freezer for 15-30 minutes, or until set. Remove from the freezer and place onto a baking sheet lined with parchment paper. Bake the burgers for about 20 minutes until firm.

Meanwhile prepare the avocado sauce. Mash the avocado and stir together with remaining ingredients until smooth. Spread the avocado sauce on the top and bottom bun, and add the beet burger.

HALIBUT FISH TACOS WITH CABBAGE AND JICAMA SLAW
Serves 4-6

INGREDIENTS

<u>For the Fish</u>
- 1 lb. fresh, wild caught halibut (can also use wild caught cod)
- 2 T extra virgin olive oil or avocado oil
- 1 T fresh lime juice
- ¼ t cumin
- ¼ t oregano
- ¼ t chili powder
- 1 T brown sugar
- 1 t sea salt, plus more to taste

<u>For the Sauce</u>
- ¼ C mayonnaise
- ¼ C sour cream
- Juice of ½ lime
- ½ jalapeño (or serrano, for more heat), diced
- 1 t chili powder

<u>For the Slaw</u>
- 1 green onion, sliced
- ¼ C red cabbage, shredded
- ¼ C jicama, peeled and shredded

<u>To Serve</u>
- Thin slices of avocado
- Diced mango
- Lime wedges
- Small white or yellow corn tortillas

DIRECTIONS

For the Halibut

Preheat the grill to 350°F. Place the halibut onto a large bed of aluminum foil. Drizzle with olive oil and lime juice. Combine the seasonings in a small bowl and rub onto the halibut. Cook the halibut for about 10-15 minutes, until the flesh flakes easily with a fork, but is still moist.

For the Sauce and Slaw

Meanwhile, prepare the sauce and slaw. Combine the mayonnaise, sour cream, lime juice, jalapeño, and chili powder together in a small bowl and set aside. Toss the shredded cabbage, shredded jicama, and green onion together in a large bowl. Prepare the remaining toppings (avocado, fruit, etc.)

For Serving

Warm the tortillas and fill with flaked halibut, slaw, sauce, and additional toppings.

WARM LENTIL SALAD WITH TOASTED WALNUTS AND GOAT CHEESE
Serves 6

INGREDIENTS
For the Salad
- 1 C baby spinach
- 1 C cooked lentils
- 2 T extra virgin olive oil
- Sea salt and black pepper, to taste
- 1 small shallot, minced
- 1/3 C toasted, coarsely chopped walnuts
- 5 oz. of goat cheese, cut into large chunks

For the Dressing
- 3 T honey
- 2 T extra virgin olive oil
- 1 T fresh lemon juice
- ½ t fresh thyme, minced
- Sea salt and black pepper, to taste

DIRECTIONS
For the Lentils
Heat 2 T of olive oil in a pot over medium-high heat. Add the shallot, and cook until tender. Add the lentils and stir until warmed, about 3-5 minutes.

For the Dressing
Meanwhile, prepare the dressing by whisking together the honey, lemon juice, thyme, olive oil, sea salt, and pepper together in a small bowl.

For Serving

Arrange the baby spinach on a large platter. Spoon the lentil and shallot mixture on top of the spinach, sprinkle with toasted walnuts and goat cheese. Use a spoon to drizzle the dressing over the top. Serve immediately.

SOMETHING FRESH

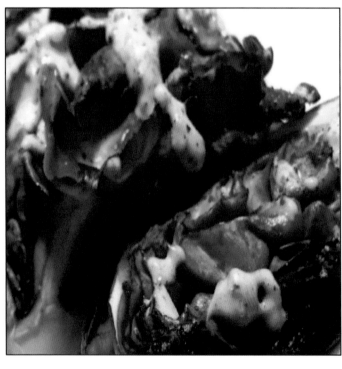

GRILLED CHICKEN SALAD
WITH CREAMY LIME DRESSING
Serves 4

INGREDIENTS
<u>For the Chicken</u>
- 2 boneless skinless chicken breasts
- ½ t paprika
- ¼ t ground cinnamon
- ¼ t ground oregano
- ¼ t ground cumin
- ½ t sea salt, to taste
- ½ of a small lemon, juiced

<u>For the Salad</u>
- 8 slices of pineapple, about ½ inch thick
- 2 sliced avocados
- ½ C baby spinach
- ¼ C macadamia nuts, toasted and coarsely chopped
- ½ C radicchio, chopped
- ½ C endive lettuce, chopped
- (Or 1 ½ C of any mixed greens you like)

<u>For the Dressing</u>
- ½ clove of garlic, minced
- ½ C plain Greek yogurt
- ¼ t crushed red pepper flakes
- 2 T olive oil
- Juice of 1 lime

DIRECTIONS

For the Spice Rub

Mix the paprika, cinnamon, oregano, cumin, salt, lime juice, and lemon juice together in a small bowl. Spread on both sides of the chicken breasts, and place in the refrigerator for at least 30 minutes, so the chicken can soak.

For the Dressing

Meanwhile, prepare the dressing. Combine the minced garlic, yogurt, red pepper flakes, oil, and lime juice and mix until smooth. Set aside.

For the Chicken

Heat the grill to medium high heat, and add the chicken breasts and pineapple slices. Cook the chicken for about 5-7 minutes per side (until no longer pink in the center), and the pineapple for 2-3 minutes per side (until you see grill marks).

For Serving

Divide the mixed greens between four plates. Top each plate with grilled pineapple, sliced avocado, sliced chicken, and macadamia nuts. Drizzle the dressing over the top.

OMEGA POWER SALAD WITH SALMON, SPINACH, AND AVOCADO
Serves 2

INGREDIENTS
For the Salad
- 8 oz. smoked salmon (or lox), roughly chopped
- 1 avocado, diced
- 3 C baby spinach
- 1 C red swiss chard, finely chopped
- ½ C strawberries, sliced
- ¼ C crumbled feta
- 1/3 C chopped toasted walnuts

For the Vinaigrette
- 3 T olive oil
- 1 ½ t fresh lemon juice
- 1 T honey
- ¼ t sea salt
- ¼ t black pepper
- 1 T chia seeds

DIRECTIONS
Gently toss all of the salad ingredients together in a large bowl until combined. In a separate bowl, whisk together the olive oil, vinegar, honey, sea salt, pepper, and chia seeds. Stir the dressing into the salad bowl and serve.

ROASTED GARLIC AND BROWN BUTTER
LENTIL SOUP
Serves 6

INGREDIENTS
- 3 T grass fed butter or coconut oil
- 1 large yellow onion, chopped
- 2 cloves garlic, minced
- ½ t crushed red pepper flakes
- 5 ½ C low sodium vegetable or chicken stock
- 4 carrots, finely chopped
- 1 ½ C lentils (dry)
- Leaves from 2 springs of fresh thyme
- ½ t cumin
- ½ t paprika
- 1/8 t turmeric
- 1/8 t ground cinnamon
- ¼ t ground coriander
- ¼ t ground ginger
- Sea salt and black pepper, to taste

DIRECTIONS
Heat the butter in a large pot over medium high heat. Add the minced garlic and toast until browned. Add the onion and carrots and sauté until softened, about 10-15 minutes.

Stir in the lentils, cumin, paprika, turmeric, coriander, ginger, red pepper flakes, cinnamon, sea salt, and black pepper. Toss for a few seconds, until combined.

Add the stock and thyme leaves. Bring to a boil, then reduce the heat and simmer for about 30 minutes, until the lentils are tender. Season to taste. Serve hot with a slice of crusty bread.

CRISPY GRILLED CABBAGE WEDGES WITH SPICY CITRUS SAUCE

Serves 8

INGREDIENTS

For the Cabbage
- 1 head of purple cabbage, cut into 8 thick wedges
- Extra virgin olive oil

For the Sauce
- ¼ C fresh lime juice
- Zest of 1 key lime
- 3 T grainy Dijon mustard
- ¼ C honey
- 1/3 C mayonnaise
- 1 clove garlic, minced
- ½ t cayenne pepper
- ½ t black pepper
- 2 t paprika

DIRECTIONS

For the Cabbage
Preheat the grill to 400°F. Remove the loose, tough, outer leaves from the cabbage and cut into 8 evenly sized wedges. Do not remove the core or stalk (this helps keep the cabbage wedges held together while they're cooking).

Brush both sides of the cabbage wedges with olive oil. Place the wedges on the grill, cover, and cook for 5-7 minutes per side, until blackened and crispy (the center of the wedge should be softened).

For the Spicy Citrus Sauce
Meanwhile, prepare the sauce. Whisk together the lime juice, lime zest, Dijon mustard, honey, mayonnaise, garlic, and seasonings.

Arrange the cabbage wedges on a large platter. Spoon the sauce over the top and serve immediately.

MID-DAY MUNCHIES

ROSEMARY ROASTED ALMONDS
Serves 6-8

INGREDIENTS

- 2 C raw, unsalted almonds
- 1 T extra-virgin olive oil
- 1 ½ t paprika
- 1 t coarse sea salt
- 1 T finely chopped fresh rosemary

DIRECTIONS

Preheat the oven to 400°F. Arrange the nuts in a single layer on a foil-lined baking sheet. Add the olive oil and seasonings (except for the salt), and toss to coat. Roast for about 10 minutes until golden. Cool to room temperature and sprinkle with coarse sea salt.

COCOA SPINACH SOOTHIE
Serves 1

INGREDIENTS
- 1 banana, cut into 1 inch slices
- 1 C firmly packed spinach, de-stemmed
- 1 ¼ C milk (almond, cow's, coconut, etc.)
- 1 T unsweetened cocoa powder
- 1T nut or seed butter (almond, cashew, peanut, sunflower seed butter, etc.)
- ¼ t pure vanilla extract
- ½ t cinnamon
- 1 T honey

DIRECTIONS
Combine all ingredients in a blender on high speed until smooth. Pour into a tall glass and enjoy.

CINNAMON SUNFLOWER SEED BUTTER

Makes About 14 oz.

INGREDIENTS

- 2 C shelled, roasted, unsalted sunflower seeds
- 2 T molasses, maple syrup, or honey
- 1 t cinnamon
- 1 t vanilla extract
- Pinch of sea salt

DIRECTIONS

Combine all ingredients in a food processor or high-powered blender until smooth, about 10 minutes. Store in an airtight jar or container in the refrigerator. Keeps for about one month.

DROP BISCUITS WITH SPINACH AND CHEDDAR
Makes 18-20 Biscuits

INGREDIENTS
- 3 C 100% whole-wheat pastry flour
- 1 T baking powder
- 2 t sea salt
- 2 C cooked spinach (can also use mustard greens or collard greens)
- 6 oz. sharp cheddar cheese, grated
- 1 ¼ C to 1 ½ C buttermilk

DIRECTIONS
Preheat the oven to 400°F. Sift the flour, baking powder, and sea salt together in a large bowl. Stir in the cheddar cheese using a fork. Stir in the cooked greens. Add 1 C of the buttermilk and stir to combine.

Continue gradually adding buttermilk and mixing, until the dough just comes together. Drop the dough onto a parchment lined baking sheet, using. Bake for 15-20 minutes until the biscuits are golden brown. Serve warm.

SOMETHING SWEET

CRANBERRY AND ORANGE PUMPKIN SEED MUFFINS
Makes 10-12 Muffins

INGREDIENTS
- 1 1/2 C almond flour (see pg. 170)
- ¾ C canned pumpkin
- ¼ C honey
- 1t baking soda
- ½ t baking powder
- ¼ t sea salt
- 1 t cinnamon
- ¼ t ginger
- 1/8 t nutmeg
- 2 t orange zest
- 1 egg
- 1/3 C shelled pumpkin seeds
- 3 T melted coconut oil or grass fed butter
- 1/3 C dried, unsweetened cranberries

DIRECTIONS
Preheat the oven to 375°F. Line a muffin pan with muffin liners or spray with nonstick spray. In a medium sized bowl, combine almond flour, baking powder, baking soda, sea salt, nutmeg, ginger, and cinnamon.

In a large bowl, whisk together the egg, pumpkin, honey, and oil or butter. Add the dry ingredient mixture, and stir until just combined. Fold in the dried cranberries and orange zest.

Pour the batter into the prepared muffin tin and gently press pumpkin seeds onto the top of each muffin. Bake for about 20-25 minutes, until an inserted toothpick comes out clean.

SOAKED BUCKWHEAT PANCAKES
Makes 8-10 Pancakes (depending on the size)

INGREDIENTS
For the Pancakes
- 1 ½ C buckwheat flour (see pg. 168)
- 1 ¼ C buttermilk
- 2 eggs, beaten
- Pinch of sea salt
- ½ t baking powder
- ½ t baking soda
- ½ t vanilla extract
- Grass fed butter or coconut oil

Topping Ideas
- Fresh mixed berries
- Maple syrup
- Raw honey
- Crispy bacon
- Grass fed butter

DIRECTIONS
Begin soaking the batter 24 hours before you plan on cooking the pancakes. Mix the buckwheat flour and buttermilk together in a large bowl until well combined. Cover and put in a warm place (on top of the fridge or near a window) for 24 hours.

When 24 hours have passed, stir in the eggs, salt, baking powder, baking soda, and vanilla. The buckwheat flour mixture may be bubbly like a sourdough bread starter. If it is, stir it down to prevent holes from forming in the pancakes. If the batter looks too dry, gradually add small amounts of buttermilk until you reach the desired consistency.

Melt butter or coconut oil in a skillet over medium high heat. Ladle about ¼ C of the batter into the skillet for each pancake. Cook for about 5 minutes, or until bubbles form and the batter starts drying slightly. Flip and cook for 2-3 minutes on the other side, until golden brown.

Place desired topping on the pancakes and serve warm.

SIX-INGREDIENT FLOURLESS PEANUT BUTTER BROWNIES

Serves 6

INGREDIENTS

- 1 C peanut butter (almond butter or sunflower seed butter also work well)
- 2 small bananas (6 oz.), mashed
- ¼ C honey
- ¼ C unsweetened cocoa powder
- 2 t baking powder
- 1 t vanilla
- 1 C dark chocolate chips or chunks (at least 65%)

DIRECTIONS

Preheat the oven to 350° F. In a large bowl, combine the peanut butter, mashed banana, honey, and vanilla until well combined. In a small bowl combine the unsweetened cocoa powder with a pinch of sea salt.

Add the dry ingredients to the wet ingredients and mix until well combined. Stir in the chocolate chips. Spread the mixture into a greased 8x10 or 9x9 baking dish. Bake for about 30-35 minutes, until an inserted toothpick comes out clean. Allow to cool before cutting and serving.

SIMPLE ALMOND CAKE
Serves 8

INGREDIENTS
- 1 ¼ C almond flour (see pg. 171)
- 2 eggs (or 3 egg whites)
- 1/3 C honey
- ¼ t almond extract
- ¼ C roughly chopped almonds
- ¼ t sea salt

DIRECTIONS
Preheat the oven to 350°F. Grease or line the bottom and sides of a loaf tin with parchment paper. In a large bowl, mix the almond flour, almond extract, and honey, until a thick paste forms.

In a small bowl, whisk together the eggs and sea salt until well beaten. Carefully fold the egg mixture into the flour mixture. Pour into the loaf tin and sprinkle the top with chopped almonds.

Bake for 20-25 minutes, until an inserted toothpick comes out clean. Allow to cool for 10 minutes. Remove from the tin and transfer to a wire rack to finish cooling. Cut into slices and serve.

DEPRESSION FIGHTING RECIPES

The following recipes incorporate the foods listed in the "Depression" section (see pg. 10) into delicious, nourishing recipes that will help you overcome depression—without the nasty side effects from prescription medication.

Rise and Shine
1. Buckwheat Porridge with Nuts, Seeds, and Fruit **(V) (VT) (GF) (DF)**
2. Smoked Salmon, Scrambled Eggs, and Avocado on Toast
3. Spicy Indian Inspired Omelette **(VT) (GF) (DF)**
4. Cakey Teff Flour Waffles with Blueberry Citrus Glaze **(V) (VT) (GF)**

Something Savory
1. Basic Bison Burgers **(DF) (GF)**
2. Pistachio and Herb Crusted Beef Tenderloin **(GF) (DF)**
3. Sesame Crusted Ahi Tuna with Lime Ginger Sauce **(GF) (DF)**
4. Chicken Soup with Spinach, Avocado, and Salsa Verde **(GF)**

Mid-Day Munchies
1. Tropical Papaya Coconut Smoothie **(V) (VT) (GF) (DF)**
2. Blueberry, Lemon, and Millet Energy Bites **(V) (VT) (GF) (DF)**
3. Whole Grain Carrot Walnut Bread **(VT) (DF)**
4. Blackberry Quinoa Bars **(VT) (GF) (DF)**

Chocoholic
1. No Bake Dark Chocolate Sunflower Seed Clusters **(VT) (GF)**
2. Dark Chocolate Rye Muffins **(VT)**
3. Chili Infused Chocolate Bark **(VT) (GF)**
4. Flourless Dark Chocolate Cake with Lavender Whipped Coconut Cream **(VT) (GF) (DF)**

Something Fresh
1. Beet Salad with Toasted Pistachios, Feta, and Citrus Vinaigrette **(VT) (GF)**
2. Grilled Broccoli and Summer Squash Salad with Sourdough Croutons **(VT)**
3. Simple Cauliflower Rice **(V) (VT) (GF) (DF)**
4. Roasted Carrots with Farro and Creamy Herb Dressing **(VT)**

RISE AND SHINE

BUCKWHEAT PORRIDGE WITH NUTS, SEEDS, AND FRUIT
Serves 4

INGREDIENTS
For the Groats
- 2 C water
- 1 C buckwheat groats (see pg.165)

Additional Topping Ideas
- Maple syrup
- Honey
- Molasses
- Ground cinnamon
- Ground ginger
- Unsweetened cocoa powder
- Vanilla extract
- Almond extract
- ¼ C milk of choice (see pg. 173-174)
- Chopped dried fruit
- Spoonful of nut or seed butter
- Chia seeds
- Flax Seeds
- Pumpkin Seeds
- Sliced almonds
- Pistachios
- Walnuts
- Unsweetened coconut flakes
- Sliced fresh fruit

DIRECTIONS
Add the water and buckwheat groats to a pot and bring to a boil. Reduce heat to a simmer, cover and cook for about 10 minutes, stirring every few

minutes, until most of the water is absorbed. The groats should be squishy, but not too watery or mushy.

Remove the groats from the heat, and add in the milk, if using. Transfer to a bowl, and stir in desired additional toppings. Serve hot.

SMOKED SALMON, SCRAMBLED EGGS, AND AVOCADO ON TOAST

Serves 2-4

INGREDIENTS

- 4 oz. thinly sliced smoked salmon (lox)
- 6 eggs
- 2 T extra virgin olive oil
- 1 T sliced green onions
- 2 T sour cream
- Pinch of sea salt and black pepper
- 1 avocado
- 1 T fresh lime juice
- 2-4 slices of toasted whole grain sourdough, rye, or pumpernickel bread

DIRECTIONS

Whisk together the eggs sea salt, and black pepper. Heat olive oil in a skillet over medium high heat. Add the eggs and cook until fluffy and just set, about 3-5 minutes. Set aside.

In a bowl, mash the avocado and lime juice together. Spread the mashed avocado over each slice of toast. Place the eggs on top of the avocado spread. Then place smoked salmon on top of the eggs. Garnish with sour cream and black pepper.

SPICY INDIAN-INSPIRED OMELETTE
Serves 1-2

INGREDIENTS

- 3-4 eggs
- 2 T milk
- 1 ½ T extra virgin olive oil
- ½ medium sized onion, finely chopped
- 1 roma tomato, finely chopped
- 2 T chopped coriander (optional)
- 1 green chili pepper, diced
- ¼ red chili pepper, diced (optional)
- Sea salt, to taste
- ½ t chili powder
- 1/8 t ground cumin

DIRECTIONS

Whisk together the eggs, sea salt, chili powder, cumin, and milk. Then add the onion, tomato, and chili peppers. Heat the olive oil in a skillet over medium-high heat.

Pour the egg mixture evenly into the pan. Once it is cooked on the bottom side, carefully flip the omelette and cook it on the other side. (You can cut the egg mixture in half and flip both halves to avoid breaking it). Garnish with fresh chopped coriander, if desired.

CAKEY TEFF FLOUR WAFFLES WITH BLUEBERRY CITRUS GLAZE
Makes 4-6 Waffles

INGREDIENTS

For the Waffles
- 2 C teff flour (see pg. 170)
- 1 ½ C milk of choice (see pg. 173-174)
- 2 T extra virgin olive oil
- 1 t baking powder
- 1 t baking soda
- Pinch of sea salt
- Pinch of cinnamon
- 2 t molasses

For the Glaze
- 2/3 C fresh blueberries
- 1/4 C fresh squeezed orange juice
- 2 t orange zest
- ½ t vanilla extract
- ¼ C maple syrup

DIRECTIONS

For the Waffles
Heat waffle iron. Spray the waffle iron with nonstick cooking spray, or coat with a thin layer of oil. Stir all of the dry ingredients together in a large bowl. Add the milk oil, and molasses, and mix until well combined. Pour the batter into the waffle iron. When the waffles have finished cooking, allow each individual waffle to cool on a wire rack (they can become mushy if stacked).

For the Blueberry Citrus Glaze

Meanwhile, prepare the glaze. Place the blueberries, orange juice, and vanilla, and pulse until smooth. Transfer to a bowl and whisk in the maple syrup and orange zest. Top waffles with glaze and serve warm.

Note: These waffles freeze very well. Just allow the waffles to cool completely and transfer to an airtight container.

SOMETHING SAVORY

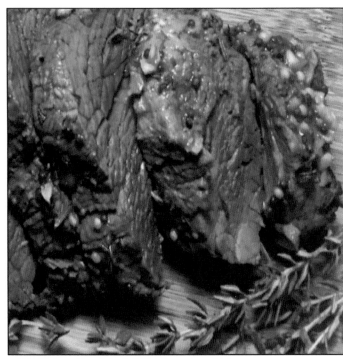

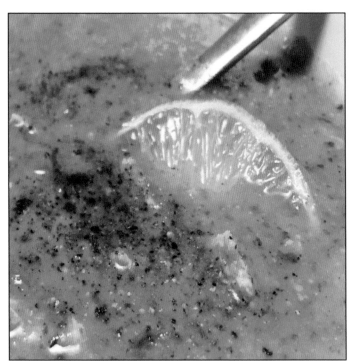

BASIC BISON BURGERS
Serves 4

INGREDIENTS
- 1 lb. of lean, grass-fed, ground bison (lean, grass-fed beef also works)
- 1 egg
- ¼ C panko breadcrumbs
- ¼ C finely chopped sweet onion
- 3 T Worcestershire sauce
- Sea salt and black pepper, to taste
- Extra virgin olive oil

DIRECTIONS
Combine all ingredients together in a large mixing bowl, and shape into 4 patties. Heat oil in a skillet over medium-high heat, and cook the patties for about 3-5 minutes per side (for medium rare). Serve on a toasted bun with desired condiments.

Note: *For a milder flavor, cook the onions in a saucepan over medium-high heat until golden brown before adding to the burger mixture.*

PISTACHIO AND HERB CRUSTED
BEEF TENDERLOIN
Serves 8-10

INGREDIENTS
- 1/3 C shelled pistachios, finely chopped
- 1 ½ t fresh thyme, chopped
- 1 T fresh rosemary, chopped
- ¼ C whole grain Dijon-mustard
- ½ t minced garlic
- ¼ C extra virgin olive oil
- Sea salt and black pepper, to taste
- Beef tenderloin roast, 2-3 pounds total (Can also use individual filet mignon steaks)

DIRECTIONS
Preheat the oven to 425°F. Season the roast with sea salt and black pepper on all sides. In a small bowl, combine the mustard, olive oil, and minced garlic. Spread the mixture evenly on all sides of the roast.

In another small bowl, mix the pistachios and herbs together. Press the pistachio mixture evenly onto the mustard layer. Put the tenderloin in a roasting pan (do not add water or liquid) and roast for about 40 minutes.

A meat thermometer will read about 135°F for medium rare, and about 150°F for medium.

SESAME CRUSTED AHI TUNA WITH LIME GINGER SAUCE
Serves 4

INGREDIENTS
<u>For the Tuna</u>
- 3 T black sesame seeds
- 3 T white sesame seeds
- 2 pieces ahi tuna (about 1 lb. total)
- ½ t wasabi paste
- 1 T oil (extra virgin or avocado works best)
- Sea salt and black pepper, to taste

<u>For the Sauce</u>
- 1 T fresh lime juice
- 1 t lime zest
- ½ t rice vinegar
- 3 T oil (extra virgin or avocado works best)
- 1 t fresh grated ginger
- ½ t minced red chili pepper (optional)

DIRECTIONS
<u>For the Tuna</u>
Pat the tuna dry and spread the wasabi paste, sea salt, and pepper on both sides. Place the sesame seeds in a small bowl. Dip the tuna into the sesame seed mixture, coating both sides.

Heat the oil in a skillet over medium-high heat. When the oil is hot, add the tuna filets, making sure they do not touch. Cook for 2 minutes on each side, and sear each edge for about 1 minute (if the seeds start browning too fast, turn down the heat). Transfer the tuna to a plate.

For the Lime Ginger Sauce

In a small bowl, whisk the lime juice, zest, rice vinegar, oil, ginger, and chili (if using) together. Thinly slice the tuna and drizzle with sauce.

CHICKEN SOUP WITH
SPINACH, AVOCADO, AND SALSA VERDE
Serves 4-6

INGREDIENTS

- 2 ripe avocados
- 3 C baby spinach, de-stemmed and chopped
- ¼ C fresh lime juice
- Sea salt, to taste
- Chili powder, to taste
- Cumin, to taste
- 2 C low sodium chicken broth
- Extra virgin olive oil
- 1 C shredded chicken (grilled or roasted)
- 2/3 C bottled salsa verde
- Sour cream (optional, for topping)

DIRECTIONS

Peel and pit the avocados and place into a food processor or blender. Add the spinach, lime juice, chicken broth, and seasonings. Pulse until you reach the desired consistency.

Heat a bit of olive oil in a pot over medium-high heat. Add the shredded chicken and the avocado mixture. Bring to a boil, then reduce heat to low and simmer for about 10 minutes. Remove from the heat, stir in the salsa verde, and season to taste. Serve with desired toppings.

MID-DAY MUNCHIES

TROPICAL PAPAYA COCONUT SMOOTHIE
Serves 4

INGREDIENTS
- 14 oz. of unsweetened coconut water
- 1 large fresh papaya, chopped and de-seeded
- ½ C pineapple chunks
- pinch of cinnamon
- Juice of 1 lime
- ½ C plain Greek yogurt

DIRECTIONS
Blend all the ingredients in a blender until smooth. Pour into tall glasses and serve with lime wedges and a sprinkle of cinnamon.

Note: Ideally, the coconut water used should NOT be from concentrate, should be unprocessed, and should not have any additives/additional ingredients. Buying a whole, young coconut and extracting the water is a good way to do this. Or, see pg. 181 for sourcing ideas.

BLUEBERRY, LEMON, AND MILLET ENERGY BITES
Makes 10- 12 Bites

INGREDIENTS
- ½ C unsweetened, pitted medjool dates (around 6)
- ½ C unsweetened dried blueberries
- ½ t vanilla extract
- ½ t almond extract
- Pinch of sea salt
- 1 C cooked millet (see pg. 166 for cooking instructions)
- 1/4 C oat flour (see pg. 170)
- Juice of ½ lemon
- Zest of ½ lemon

DIRECTIONS
Line a small, shallow baking dish or tupperware container with wax paper. Combine all ingredients in a food processor until the mixture clumps together. Roll the mixture into 12 balls. Sprinkle additional lemon zest over the top of each ball. Place in the refrigerator (for about 2 hours) or freezer (for about 1 hour) until firm. Store in an airtight container in the refrigerator.

WHOLE GRAIN CARROT WALNUT BREAD
Serves 8

INGREDIENTS
For the Dry Mixture
- 2 C 100% Whole Wheat Flour
- ½ t baking soda
- ½ t baking powder
- 2 t cinnamon
- 1/8 t nutmeg
- ¼ t ginger
- Pinch of sea salt
- 1 T orange zest
- 1 T lemon zest
- 1 C roughly chopped walnuts

For the Wet Mixture
- 1 ½ C grated carrots
- 1/2 C honey, plus more for drizzling
- ½ ripe banana
- 1/2 C milk of choice (see pg. 173-174)
- 2 T extra virgin olive oil
- 1 t vanilla extract
- 1 egg

DIRECTIONS
Preheat the oven to 350°F. In a large bowl, combine the flour, ¾ of the walnuts, baking soda, baking powder, spices, sea salt, orange zest, and lemon zest.

In a separate bowl, combine the grated carrot, honey, milk, oil, vanilla, and egg. Add the wet ingredients to the dry ingredients and mix until well combined.

Line a 9"x13" loaf pan with parchment paper and pour in the mixture. Sprinkle the remaining chopped walnuts over the top, and drizzle with honey.

Bake for about 50 minutes, until an inserted toothpick comes out clean. Let cool for about 15 minutes in the loaf tin. Then remove from the tin and transfer to a tray or platter to finish cooling.

BLACKBERRY QUINOA BARS
Makes 12 Bars

INGREDIENTS
<u>For the Dry Mixture</u>
- 1 ¼ C rolled oats
- 1 C cooked quinoa (any color, see pg. 165 for cooking instructions, remembering to rinse dry quinoa before cooking)
- 1 t baking powder
- Pinch of sea salt
- ½ t cinnamon
- ¼ C seeds of choice (hemp, pumpkin, and flax work well)

<u>For the Wet Mixture</u>
- 1/3 C maple syrup
- 1 C mashed banana
- 2 eggs
- 1 t vanilla extract
- 1 ½ C fresh blackberries
- 2 T fresh lemon juice
- 2 T nut or seed butter of choice

DIRECTIONS
Preheat the oven to 350°F. Line a 9"x9" baking sheet with parchment paper. Spray both sides with non-stick cooking spray. In a large mixing bowl, combine the oats, quinoa, baking powder, sea salt, cinnamon, and seeds.

In a separate bowl, combine the banana, nut butter, eggs, vanilla, and lemon juice. Add the wet ingredients to the dry ingredients and mix until fully combined. Gently fold in the blackberries.

Put the batter into the prepared baking sheet and smooth with a spatula. Bake for 20-30 minutes, until firm and golden brown. Remove from the oven and allow to cool completely in the pan. Once cool, slice into squares. Store in an airtight container.

CHOCOHOLIC

NO BAKE DARK CHOCOLATE SUNFLOWER SEED CLUSTERS
Makes 20 Clusters

INGREDIENTS
- 12 oz. dark chocolate (at least 65%), melted
- 2 C roasted, unsalted sunflower seeds
- 1 C puffed brown rice cereal
- 1 t vanilla extract
- 2 T honey
- Pinch of sea salt

DIRECTIONS
Line a baking sheet with aluminum foil and set aside. Place the sunflower seeds, brown rice cereal, and sea salt in a large bowl.

Melt the chocolate until smooth. Pour over the dry ingredients. Add honey and vanilla, and stir with a spatula until everything is well combined and coated in chocolate.

Drop the mixture by large spoonfuls onto the baking sheet. Refrigerate for 20-30 minutes until set. Store in a parchment lined airtight container.

DARK CHOCOLATE RYE MUFFINS
Makes 12 Muffins

INGREDIENTS
<u>For the Dry Mixture</u>
- 2 C whole grain dark rye flour (see pg. 168)
- 5 ½ T unsweetened cocoa powder
- ½ t sea salt
- 2 t baking powder
- 1 t baking soda

<u>For the Wet Mixture</u>
- ½ t vanilla extract
- 3 eggs
- 1 C milk of choice (see pg. 173-174)
- 2/3 C extra virgin olive oil
- 2/3 C pure maple syrup
- ½ C of dark chocolate (at least 75%), coarsely chopped

DIRECTIONS
Preheat the oven to 400°F. Prepare a muffin tin with paper liners. Sift together the flours, cocoa powder, salt, baking powder, and baking soda together in a medium bowl.

In a separate bowl, beat the eggs, milk, vanilla extract, olive oil, and maple syrup. Add the dry ingredient mixture to the wet ingredients, and stir until well combined. Carefully fold in the chopped chocolate with a spatula. Pour the batter into the muffin tins, and bake for about 18 minutes, until an inserted toothpick comes out clean.

CHILI INFUSED CHOCOLATE BARK
Makes 20-24 Pieces

INGREDIENTS
- 12 oz. dark chocolate (at least 70%)
- 2 T unsweetened cocoa powder
- 1 T cinnamon
- 1 T paprika
- 2 t cayenne pepper
- 1 T chili powder
- ½ t sea salt
- ½ C crushed cashews

DIRECTIONS
Line a baking dish with wax paper. Melt chocolate until smooth. Add in cocoa powder, spices, cashews, and stir until combined. Pour the chocolate mixture onto the baking pan and spread evenly. Sprinkle additional spices or crushed cashews on top if desired. Place in the freezer for 20 minutes, until set. Break into pieces and store in an airtight container.

FLOURLESS DARK CHOCOLATE CAKE WITH LAVENDER WHIPPED COCONUT CREAM

Serves 6

INGREDIENTS

For the Cake

- 5 oz. dark chocolate (at least 70%), roughly chopped
- 1/2 C grass fed butter or coconut oil
- 3 eggs
- Pinch of sea salt
- ½ t vanilla extract
- ¼ C unsweetened cocoa powder
- ¾ C honey

For the Lavender Whipped Coconut Cream

- 1-13.5 oz can coconut milk, refrigerated overnight
- 1/8 t finely minced lavender flowers or lavender extract

DIRECTIONS

For the Cake

Preheat the oven to 375°F. Thoroughly grease an 8" spring-form pan with butter or coconut oil. Line with parchment paper if desired. Melt the dark chocolate and butter/coconut oil together until smooth.

In a separate bowl, whisk the cocoa powder, honey, vanilla, eggs, and sea salt. Pour this mixture into the melted chocolate and stir until well combined. Transfer to the greased cake pan and smooth the top.

Bake for about 25 minutes, until the center is firm. Allow to cool in the pan for 15 minutes. Remove the sides of the pan and cool completely.

For the Lavender Whipped Coconut Cream

Chill a mixing bowl in the freezer for 15-20 minutes. Flip the can of coconut cream upside down (without shaking), and open the can from the bottom.

Pour out the coconut water (saving for future use if desired). Now you are left with pure coconut cream. Put the coconut cream into the chilled mixing bowl, and, with a stand mixer or hand mixer, whip until soft peaks form. Gradually add the lavender, and whip until fully combined. Serve with the cake.

Notes:
Add the lavender gradually, and taste as you go along so that you can avoid adding too much.

To make a traditional whipped cream, use 1 ½ C of heavy whipping cream instead of coconut cream

Try using orange, rose, almond, or vanilla extract in place of lavender if you want a different taste.

SOMETHING FRESH

BEET SALAD WITH TOASTED PISTACHIOS, FETA, AND CITRUS VINAIGRETTE

Serves 4-6

INGREDIENTS
- 4 medium beets (any color), peeled and cut into large chunks
- 1/3 C shelled, unsalted pistachios
- ¼ C crumbled feta cheese
- 2 T fresh lemon juice
- 1 T extra virgin olive oil
- Sea salt and black pepper, to taste

DIRECTIONS
Place the beet chunks in a large pot of water and bring to a boil. Reduce the heat and simmer until just fork tender. Drain and cool to room temperature.

Heat the pistachios in a small saucepan over medium heat, and toast until fragrant and golden brown. Set aside.

In a small bowl, whisk together the olive oil, lemon juice, sea salt, and black pepper.

Place the cooled beets in a large salad bowl and pour over the olive oil mixture. Sprinkle the feta cheese and pistachios on top, and toss gently.

GRILLED BROCCOLI AND SUMMER SQUASH SALAD WITH SOURDOUGH CROUTONS

Serves 4-6

INGREDIENTS

For the Salad
- 3 yellow squash, sliced into ½-inch thick rounds
- 1 large head of broccoli, cut into florets
- ¼ C unsalted, toasted pine nuts

For the Sourdough Croutons
- Four ½ inch slices of good quality, crusty sourdough bread
- Extra virgin olive oil
- Dried thyme, to taste
- Paprika, to taste

For the Dressing
- 3 T fresh lemon juice
- ½ C mayonnaise
- 2 T plain yogurt
- ¼ C extra virgin olive oil
- Sea salt and black pepper, to taste
- 1 t crushed red pepper flakes
- 1 clove of garlic, minced

DIRECTIONS

For the Dressing
In a medium bowl, combine the lemon juice, mayonnaise, yogurt, olive oil, garlic, and seasonings. Set aside.

For the Croutons

Cut the bread into cubes and place on a baking sheet. Drizzle with olive oil, and sprinkle with paprika and dried thyme. Toss to coat. Bake at 400°F for about 10 minutes, or until golden brown. Remove from the oven and let cool.

For the Vegetables

Toss the broccoli florets with olive oil and wrap into a packet of aluminum foil. Grill for about 15 minutes, or until fork tender.

Heat the grill to medium-high and brush the rack lightly with olive oil. Brush both sides of the squash slices with olive oil, and arrange across the grill grate. Grill for about 3-5 minutes on each side, until tender and nicely browned.

For Serving

Place the broccoli, squash and pine nuts in a large salad bowl. Pour the dressing over the top and toss to coat. Sprinkle the croutons on top and serve.

SIMPLE CAULIFLOWER RICE
Serves 4

INGREDIENTS
- 1 large head of cauliflower, cut into florets
- Extra virgin olive oil
- Sea salt, black pepper, and additional seasonings, to taste

DIRECTIONS
Place the cauliflower florets into a food processor and pulse until finely chopped (it should have a rice-like texture). Heat oil in a pot or skillet over medium-high heat. Add the cauliflower, and cook until golden brown. Season to taste with desired spices.

Note: This is great to use in place of rice in a stir-fry or curry-based dish.

ROASTED CARROTS WITH FARRO AND CREAMY HERB DRESSING
Serves 4

INGREDIENTS
For the Farro
- 1 C dry farro, rinsed (see pg. 167)
- 1 t fresh lemon juice
- 1 t extra virgin olive oil
- ½ t sea salt

For the Carrots
- 1 lb. of carrots (preferably heirloom variety), cut in half lengthwise (if using standard carrots, cut into ¼ -inch thick strips)
- ½ t paprika
- ¼ t cumin
- ¼ t cinnamon
- Pinch of ground ginger
- ½ t sea salt

For the Dressing
- 1/3 C sour cream
- 2 T plain yogurt
- ½ t lemon zest
- 1 clove of garlic, minced
- 2 T fresh, minced parsley
- 2 t fresh, minced chives
- ½ t sea salt
- ½ t black pepper

Toppings
- ¼ C pumpkin seeds, toasted

DIRECTIONS

For the Dressing

In a small bowl, combine the sour cream, yogurt, lemon zest, and herbs. Set aside.

For the Farro

In a saucepan over medium-high heat, combine the farro with 3 C water. Bring to a boil, reduce the heat to simmer, and cook for 20-30 minutes. The farro will be tender and slightly chewy when cooked.

Drain off the water and put the farro back into the pot. Add the olive oil, lemon juice, and salt, stirring well to combine. Cover and set aside.

For the Carrots

Meanwhile, prepare the carrots. Preheat the oven to 425°F. Place the carrots on a rimmed, parchment-lined baking sheet. Drizzle with olive oil and sprinkle with seasonings. Roast for 20-30 minutes, until fork tender and nicely browned.

For the Pumpkin Seeds

In a skillet over medium-high heat, toast the pumpkin seeds until golden brown. (You will hear a "popping" noise). Remove from the heat and set aside.

For Serving

Pour the farro onto a large platter. Arrange the carrots on top, and drizzle with dressing. Sprinkle all over with toasted pumpkin seeds. Serve warm or at room temperature.

INSOMNIA FIGHTING SNACKS

The following recipes incorporate the foods listed in the "Insomnia" section (see pg. 17) into delicious, nourishing recipes that will help you overcome insomnia—without the nasty side effects from prescription medication. Try eating one of these snacks a few hours before bed.

1. Whole Wheat Banana Nut Muffins **(VT) (DF)**
2. Fig, Vanilla, and Walnut Bars **(VT) (GF)**
3. No Bake Ginger Cookies **(V) (GF) (VT) (DF)**
4. Simple Tart Cherry Sorbet **(V) (VT) (GF) (DF)**
5. Maple-Sweetened Cashew and Macadamia Nut Butter **(V) (VT) (GF) (DF)**

WHOLE WHEAT BANANA NUT MUFFINS
Makes 8-12 Muffins

INGREDIENTS

Dry

- 1 C 100% whole-wheat flour
- ½ C hazelnut or oat flour (see pg. 170-171)
- 1 ½ t baking powder
- ¼ t baking soda
- Pinch of sea salt
- ½ t cinnamon
- 1/3 C chopped hazelnuts

Wet

- 3 large bananas, mashed
- 2 eggs
- 2 T softened grass fed butter or coconut oil
- 1/3 C honey
- 1 t vanilla extract
- 1 t almond extract

DIRECTIONS

Preheat the oven to 350°F. Grease or line a muffin tin with paper baking cups. In a large bowl, mix the bananas, eggs, honey, butter/oil, and extracts. In a separate bowl, sift together the flours, baking powder baking soda, sea salt, and cinnamon. Add the dry ingredient mixture to the wet ingredient mixture and stir until just combined. Carefully fold in the chopped hazelnuts.

Pour into the muffin tin and bake for 20-25 minutes, until an inserted toothpick comes out clean. Allow to cool in the pan for about 5 minutes, then transfer to a wire rack to finish cooling.

FIG, VANILLA, AND WALNUT BARS
Makes about 12 Bars

INGREDIENTS
For the Base
- ½ C chopped walnuts
- ¼ C chopped almonds
- 2 T chopped pistachios
- ½ C unsweetened dried figs
- ¼ C unsweetened medjool dates (pit removed)
- ¼ C unsweetened dried apricots
- 1 T water
- ½ t vanilla extract
- 1 t cinnamon

For the Top Layer
- 5 T plain Greek yogurt
- Cinnamon, for sprinkling

DIRECTIONS
Combine all of the ingredients for the base in a food processor until the mixture clumps together. Line a rectangular tupperware container with wax paper. Pour the mixture into the container and press down into a flat, even layer. Freeze for about 30-45 minutes, until set.

Once the base has set, spread the yogurt on top into a flat, even layer. Sprinkle cinnamon over the top.

Put back in the freezer for about 1 hour, until set.

Remove from the freezer and slice into bars. Store in an airtight container in the freezer.

NO BAKE GINGER COOKIES
Makes About 20 Cookies

INGREDIENTS
- 1 C dried figs, packed (stems removed)
- 1 C crunchy almond butter
- 1 C rolled oats
- 2 T fresh ginger root, peeled and grated
- 3 T blackstrap molasses
- ½ t cinnamon
- ¼ t nutmeg
- 1/8 t cloves
- Pinch of sea salt

DIRECTIONS
Line a baking sheet or glass baking dish with wax paper. Place the figs in a food processor and pulse until finely chopped. Add the almond butter and process until well combined. Add the oats and pulse until a dough-like consistency forms and clumps together in a ball. Break the ball apart and add all remaining ingredients. Pulse to combine.

Wet your hands, form the dough into balls and press down into cookie shapes. Place the cookies onto the baking sheet and freeze for about 20 minutes until set. Store in the fridge (keeps for a few weeks) or freezer (keeps for a few months).

SIMPLE TART CHERRY SORBET
Serves 6

INGREDIENTS
- 4 C pitted tart cherries
- 1 C water
- ¼ C coconut sugar
- ½ t sea salt
- ½ t almond extract

DIRECTIONS
Puree the cherries, water, coconut sugar, sea salt, and almond extract in a blender until smooth. Strain through a sieve (this helps get rid of large chunks). Pour into an airtight container and freeze until firm.

MAPLE-SWEETEND CASHEW
AND MACADAMIA NUT BUTTER
Makes About 2 Cups

INGREDIENTS
- 2 C whole, unsalted macadamia nuts
- 1 C chopped, unsalted cashews
- 2 T extra virgin olive oil
- ½ C pure maple syrup
- 2 t vanilla extract
- ½ t sea salt
- ½ t cinnamon

DIRECTIONS
Pulse the macadamia nuts and cashews together in a food processor for about 5 minutes, until smooth. Add the sea salt, vanilla, maple syrup, cinnamon, and olive oil (you may need to add more olive oil, depending on the consistency). Puree until smooth and incorporated. Season to taste. Remove from the food processor and transfer to an airtight container (a glass mason jar works well).

FATIGUE FIGHTING SNACKS

The following recipes incorporate the foods listed in the "Fatigue" section (see pg.24) into delicious, nourishing recipes that will help you overcome fatigue.

1. Energizing Banana Smoothie **(VT) (V) (GF) (DF)**
2. Iron Man Kitchen Sink Cookies **(VT) (V) (GF) (DF)**
3. Energy Boosting Wellness Shot **(VT) (V) (GF) (DF)**
4. Sea Salt and Dark Chocolate Dipped Orange Slices **(VT) (V) (GF)**
5. Honey, Lemon, and Poppy Seed Power Muffins **(VT) (GF) (DF)**

ENERGIZING BANANA SMOOTHIE
Serves 1

INGREDIENTS
- 1 C almond milk
- 2 T blackstrap molasses
- ½ t cinnamon
- ¼ t unsweetened cocoa powder
- ½ t vanilla extract
- ½ t almond extract
- 1 frozen banana
- 1 T chia seeds

DIRECTIONS
Place all of the ingredients into a blender and puree until smooth. Add spices and/or molasses to taste.

IRON MAN KITCHEN SINK COOKIES
Makes About 20 Cookies

INGREDIENTS

Dry
- 2 ½ C almond flour (see pg. 171)
- ½ t sea salt
- ½ C shelled, unsalted sunflower seeds
- ½ C dried apricots, chopped
- ½ C dark chocolate chips (at least 60%)

Wet
- ½ t vanilla extract
- 7 T pure maple syrup
- 3 T blackstrap molasses
- 1 egg
- 1/3 C coconut oil or melted grass fed butter

DIRECTIONS

Preheat the oven to 350°F. Line a baking sheet with parchment paper. Combine the dry ingredients together in a large bowl. Whisk the vanilla, egg, maple syrup, molasses, and oil/butter in a small bowl. Pour the wet mixture into the dry mixture and stir until fully combined.

Scoop out into rounded spoonfuls and press down to flatten on the baking sheet. Bake for 15-20 minutes, until golden brown. Remove to a wire rack to cool.

ENERGY BOOSTING WELLNESS SHOT
Serves 1

INGREDIENTS

- 1 oz. of unsweetened beetroot juice
- Juice of ½ a lime
- 2 oz. of unsweetened coconut water
- Juice of 10 strawberries
- ¼ t cinnamon

DIRECTIONS

Place the beetroot juice, lime juice, coconut water, strawberry juice, and cinnamon into a blender. Mix until well combined. Pour into a shot glass

SEA SALT AND DARK CHOCOLATE DIPPED ORANGE SLICES
Serves 6

INGREDIENTS
- 2 navel oranges
- 8 oz. dark chocolate (at least 60%)
- Coarse sea salt

DIRECTIONS
Peel the oranges and separate them into segments. Line a platter with wax paper. Melt the dark chocolate until smooth. Dip the orange slices in the chocolate about half way up, and place on the parchment paper. Sprinkle with coarse sea salt while the chocolate is still wet. Place in the refrigerator for about 30 minutes, or in the freezer for about 15-20 minutes, until set.

HONEY, LEMON, AND
POPPY SEED POWER MUFFINS
Makes 8-12 Muffins

INGREDIENTS

Dry

- 1 ¼ C oat flour (see pg. 170)
- ½ t sea salt
- 1 T poppy seeds
- ½ t baking powder
- ½ t baking soda

Wet

- 6T honey
- 2 ½ T fresh lemon juice
- ½ T lemon zest
- ½ C plain yogurt
- 1 t vanilla extract
- 1 large egg

DIRECTIONS

Preheat the oven to 350°F. Thoroughly grease a muffin tin with non-stick spray (these muffins will stick to paper liners). In a large bowl, mix the egg, vanilla, yogurt, lemon juice, and lemon zest until well combined.

In a separate bowl, combine the oat flour, salt, baking powder, baking soda, and chia seeds. Gradually add the dry mixture to the wet mixture, stirring until well incorporated. Pour the batter into the muffin tins, and bake for 15-20 minutes, until an inserted toothpick comes out clean. Let cool, and transfer to an airtight container.

GUT HEALING SNACKS

The following recipes incorporate the foods listed in the "Gut Health" section (see pg. 28) into delicious, nourishing recipes that will help you overcome digestive issues.

1. Bone Broth 101 **(GF) (DF)**
2. Basic Fermented Veggies **(VT) (V) (GF) (DF)**
3. Overnight Refrigerator Pickles **(VT) (V) (GF) (DF)**
4. Ginger Chews **(VT) (V) (GF) (DF)**
5. Two Ingredient Pineapple Whip **(VT) (GF)**

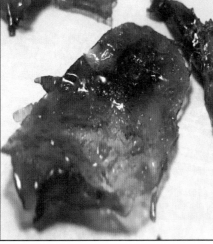

BONE BROTH 101
Amount Made Varies

INGREDIENTS
Bones (choose one of the following options)
- 1 chicken carcass
- 1 turkey carcass
- 1 fish carcass
- 2 to 3 lbs. of beef soup bones
- 2 to 3 lbs. of pork soup bones
- 2 to 3 lbs. of lamb soup bones

Vegetable Additions (optional, use as much or as little as you like)
- Large onion, peeled and cut into quarters
- Cloves of garlic, peeled and minced
- Carrots, broken into thirds
- Celery ribs, broken into thirds
- Handful of fresh herbs (rosemary, thyme, parsley, etc.)

Liquid
1-2 T apple cider vinegar (this helps the bones release minerals into the water, flavoring the broth)
Enough water to completely cover the amount of bones you have in the pot (this varies depending on the amount of bones you're using)

DIRECTIONS
In a large pot, place the bones, water, and vinegar. Let this sit for 30-60 minutes—DO NOT turn on the heat (this allows the bones to release minerals into the water). Add any vegetables you're using to the pot. Put the pot over medium-high heat and bring to a boil. Turn the heat to the lowest setting, cover and let cook for 6-8 hours.

When the broth has finished cooking, remove the lid and skim off any foam from the top. Strain the bones, vegetables, and herbs out of the pot (transfer the vegetables to a separate bowl and refrigerate for later use). Let the broth cool. Place the lid back onto the pot and put the broth in the freezer for about 3 hours.

Remove the broth from the freezer, and, using a large spoon, remove the layer of fat from the top. Transfer to an airtight container and return to the fridge, where it will keep for about a week—or to the freezer, where it will keep for about a month.

Note: To make bone broth in a crockpot, place bones, vegetables/herbs, water, and apple cider vinegar in the crockpot, turn to the low setting, cover, and let cook for 6-8 hours.

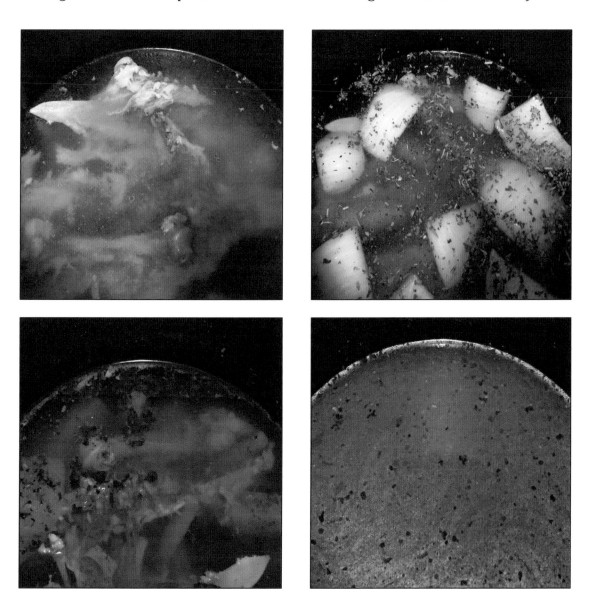

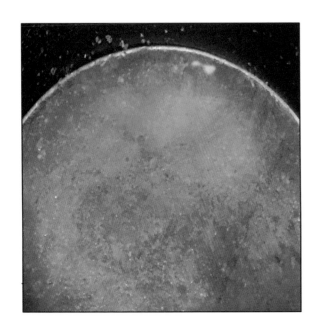

BASIC FERMENTED VEGGIES
Serves 8

INGREDIENTS

- 2-3 T sea salt or kosher salt
- 1 quart of water
- 2 C carrots cut into thin short slices
- 1 C small cauliflower florets
- 1 clove of garlic, minced and peeled
- ½ t coriander seeds
- ¼ t black peppercorn

DIRECTIONS

Combine salt and water, stirring until the salt dissolves. Place the vegetables, garlic, coriander, and peppercorn in a half-gallon mason jar. Pour the saltwater over the vegetables, leaving at least 1 inch of headspace at the top of the jar. Place an airtight lid on the jar and seal tightly.

Leave the jar out at room temperature, to ferment. Twice a day, lift the lid and release the carbon dioxide gas that is being created. After 3 days, the vegetables will be tangy, crunchy, and ready to eat. Store in the refrigerator.

Note: Make sure to use sea salt or kosher salt. Salt that is iodized will prevent the vegetables from fermenting.

OVERNIGHT REFRIGERATOR PICKLES
Serves 12-20

INGREDIENTS
- 1 ½ C distilled white vinegar
- 2 C water
- 2 T raw cane sugar (you can also use coconut sugar)
- 1 t whole mustard seeds (coriander seeds work too)
- 1 t whole peppercorns (any color)
- 3 cloves of minced garlic
- 2 t sea salt
- fresh sprigs of dill (optional)
- 6 cucumbers, thinly sliced

DIRECTIONS
Place the water, vinegar, sugar, mustard seeds, peppercorn, garlic and salt in a pot to make a brine. Bring to a boil, then reduce the heat and simmer for 1-2 minutes. Remove from the heat.

Fill glass mason jars about ¾ full with the cucumber slices and fresh sprigs of dill (if using). Pour the brine into the mason jars, until the cucumbers are covered, leaving about ¼ to ½ inch of room at the top of the jar. Cover and seal the jars, refrigerate overnight, and enjoy.

GINGER CHEWS
Makes About 20 Chews (depending on size)

INGREDIENTS
- 2 C water
- 1 C fresh ginger root, peeled and very thinly sliced (a vegetable peeler works well for slicing)
- ½ C honey
- ½ t fresh lemon zest

DIRECTIONS
Line a small glass-baking dish with wax paper. Place the ginger and water in a saucepan and bring to a boil. Cover and reduce the heat to a simmer, for about 30 minutes.

Remove the lid, and simmer, uncovered for an additional 10 minutes. Drain all but ¼ C of water from the pot. Add the honey and lemon zest. Simmer, uncovered over low heat for about 20 minutes, stirring occasionally. The ginger will become darker and the honey will thicken and for a caramel-like coating.

Take off the heat, and remove the ginger pieces using a fork. Transfer to the baking sheet to cool. Once cool, use a paper towel to gently blot off excess glaze.

Store in an airtight container for 4-6 weeks.

TWO INGREDIENT PINEAPPLE WHIP
Serves 4

INGREDIENTS
- 4 C frozen pineapple chunks
- 1 C plain yogurt (preferably whole milk or 2%)

DIRECTIONS
Place the pineapple and yogurt in a food processor or blender on high speed for 1-2 minutes. Serve immediately.

Appendix

Food Cravings Chart

CRAVING	YOU MAY NEED	CAN BE FOUND IN FOODS SUCH AS
Chocolate	Magnesium	Almonds, cocoa, dark chocolate, avocados, swiss chard, spinach, yogurt
Sweets	Chromium	Broccoli, grapes, tomatoes, onions, romaine lettuce, wheat germ, oranges
	Carbohydrates	Fresh fruits, whole grains, root vegetables
	Phosphorous	Chicken, beef, fish, eggs, nuts, legumes, yogurt, cheeses
	Sulfur	Cranberries, horseradish, cabbage, cauliflower, brussels sprouts
Bread	Nitrogen	Fish, chicken, pork, beef, nuts, beans
Oily Foods	Calcium	Beet greens, mustard greens, yogurt, cheeses, sesame seeds
	Phosphorous	Chicken, beef, fish, eggs, yogurt, cheeses, onion, broccoli, brussels sprouts
Caffeine	Sulfur	Cranberries, horseradish, cabbage, cauliflower, brussels sprouts
	Sodium	Unrefined sea salt, apple cider vinegar, coconut water, mineral water
	Iron	Lean red meat, black cherries, oats, dark chocolate
	Protein	Meat, poultry, fish, nuts, eggs, yogurt, cheeses
Alcohol	Vitamin C	Citrus fruits, broccoli, tomatoes, papayas
	Calcium	Beet greens, mustard greens, yogurt, cheeses, sesame seeds
	Glutamine	Lean beef, pork, chicken, turkey, spinach, cabbage, parsley
	Potassium	Bananas, sweet potatoes, potatoes, swiss chard, apricots, avocado, cantaloupe
Chewing Ice	Iron	Lean beef, black cherries, oats, dark chocolate
Burnt Food	Carbohydrates	Fresh fruits, whole grains, root vegetables
Soda	Calcium	Beet greens, mustard greens, yogurt, cheeses, sesame seeds
Salty Foods	Chloride	Goat cheese, fish, unrefined sea salt
Acidic Foods	Magnesium	Almonds, cocoa, dark chocolate, avocados, swiss chard, spinach, yogurt
Cold Drinks	Manganese	Walnuts, almonds, pecans, pineapple, blueberries
Overeating	Hydration	Water, coconut water, watermelon, cucumber, celery, strawberries
	Silicon	100% whole grain bread, wheat bran, dried fruits, root vegetables
Lack of Appetite	Vitamin B1	Nuts and seeds, beans, organ meats
	Vitamin B3	Halibut, beef, tuna, turkey, pork, seeds and legumes
	Manganese	Walnuts, almonds, pecans, pineapple, blueberries
	Chloride	Goat cheese, fish, unrefined sea salt
Tobacco	Silicon	100% whole grain bread, wheat bran, dried fruits, root vegetables
	Tyrosine	Turkey, yogurt, peanuts, sesame seeds, pumpkin seeds, cheeses

Herbs Chart

HERB	WHAT IT LOOKS LIKE	POTENTIAL BENEFIT	HOW TO USE IT
Parsley		Used to treat UTI's Used to treat bladder infections Used to treat kidney infections Used to treat PMS symptoms Used to settle an upset stomach	Garnish soup Chop and add to sour cream Chop and add to salsa Use to make Chimichurri sauce Sprinkle on top of roasted veggies
Tarragon		Used in easing toothaches Used to ease PMS symptoms Used to settle an upset stomach	Use to season a roasted chicken Add to a vinaigrette Use in a classic French steak sauce
Dill		Used to treat insomnia Used to settle an upset stomach Used to treat colic in infants	Stir into cream cheese and add to salmon-topped crackers Add to homemade pickles
Basil		Antibacterial properties Antimicrobial properties Used to stimulate appetite	Caprese Salad Add to bruschetta Use as a pizza topping
Lavender		Used to promote sleep and relaxation Used to improve circulation Used to stimulate appetite	Add to cookies, scones, and other desserts Use to create Herbs de Provence seasoning
Oregano		Used to ease common cold symptoms (cough and stuffy nose) Anitmicrobial properties Used to ease PMS symptoms	Add to a Mexican-inspired spice rub Infuse into olive oil Use to make herb crusted goat cheese

Sage		Used to reduce inflammation Used to stimulate appetite	Use to season a roasted chicken Pan-fry and use as a garnish for butternut squash soup
Rosemary		Used topically to treat eczema Used to treat high blood pressure Used to treat rheumatism Used to ease headaches	Infuse into olive oil Use to season a roasted chicken Use to season roasted potatoes and root vegetables Combine with chocolate for a new take on desserts Add to shortbread cookies for an Italian twist
Peppermint		Used with honey to treat sore throats Used to ease cold symptoms (sinus pressure, stuffy nose) Used to treat liver issues Used to improve energy levels Used to treat colic	Try peppermint tea Use as a garnish for roast lamb Use as a garnish for fruit salad Stir into yogurt sauce/dressing Add to chilled soup
Thyme		Used to treat kidney issues Used to lower cholesterol Antifungal properties Used to treat high blood pressure	Use to season a roasted chicken Add to homemade bone broths Use as a seasoning for roasted veggies Make lemon-thyme bars
Cilantro		Antibacterial Properties Used to treat heavy metal toxicity Antioxidant Properties Used to help stabilize blood sugar	Add to salsa and guacamole Use as a garnish on Mexican inspired dishes Add to salad dressings
Marjoram		Antiviral properties Antifungal properties Used to help calm an upset stomach Used to help relieve PMS symptoms	Use to season roasted meats Use as a garnish for roasted veggies Add to egg-based dishes

Spices Chart

SPICE	WHAT IT LOOKS LIKE	POTENTIAL BENEFIT	HOW TO USE IT
Cardamom		Used to help prevent cancer Used to help prevent blood clots Used to treat intestinal infections Used to ease an upset stomach	Add to garam masala Sprinkle into a chai tea latte Incorporate into your favorite spiced cookies, cakes, or breads
Cinnamon		Anti-inflammatory properties Helps stabilize blood sugar Used to help regulate blood pressure Antibacterial properties Antifungal properties Improves insulin sensitivity	Sprinkle into your morning porridge Sprinkle onto sliced apples Sprinkle into coffee or tea Use to season roasted carrots, yams, or sweet potatoes Use to season roasted nuts or homemade nut/seed butters
Turmeric		Anti-inflammatory properties Used to help treat and prevent cancer Used to help ease arthritis symptoms Used to ease an upset stomach	Add to garam masala Add to Indian inspired curries Sprinkle into brewed tea
Cumin		Used to help prevent diabetes Used to ease an upset stomach Used to help prevent cancer Antioxidant properties	Add to Mexican inspired spice rubs Sprinkle into Guacamole
Nutmeg		Used to help improve liver function Used to help imrove liver function Used to help treat insomnia Used to ease an upset stomach	Add to spiced baked goods Add to a season steak rub Sprinkle into a pumpkin smoothie Sprinkle into butternut squash soup
Cayenne Pepper		Antifungal properties Used to help clear sinuses Helps stabilize blood sugar Helps improve circulation	Use to season roasted nuts Add to homemade chocolate bark for a spicy twist

Ginger		Anti-inflammatory properties Used to help treat and prevent cancer Helps relieve nausea Helps relieve symptoms of indigestion	Add to spiced baked goods Mince and add to stir-frys Sprinkle into brewed green tea Try a carrot, ginger, and turmeric smoothie
Cloves		Anti-viral properties Anti-bacterial properties Helps stabilize blood sugar levels Applied topically to treat acne Used to help prevent heart disease	Add to spiced baked goods Add to homemade apple cider Sprinkle into fruit compotes
Paprika		Anti-inflammatory properties Anti-bacterial properties Helps improve circulation Used to help stimulate digestion	Use to season roasted meats Used to season roasted veggies Add to roasted nuts
Peppercorn (Black) (Green) (White) (Red)		Anti-bacterial properties Used to help stimulate digestion Used to help clear sinuses Used to help prevent cancer	Use to season roasted meats Use to season roasted veggies Add whole peppercorns to brines for chicken or turkey
Crushed Red Pepper (Red Pepper Flakes)		Used to help clear sinuses Used to help stimulate digestion Anti-cancer properties Used to boost the immune system	Add to remoulade sauce for an a added kick Sprinkle into soups Sprinkle into a mixture of honey, salt, olive oil, and lime juice for a spicy marinade
Vanilla		Anti-inflammatory properties Used to help prevent cancer Used to help ease nausea Used to help reduce anxiety	Incorporate fresh vanilla bean into homemade whipped cream Add 1/2 teaspoon of vanilla extract to plain yogurt to create flavor without extra sugar

Salts Table

NAME	WHAT IT LOOKS LIKE	DESCRIPTION
Himalayan Sea Salt		Extracted by hand from natural salt mines in the Himalayan mountain range Commerical supply also comes from the mountainous regions of Pakistan
Alaea Red Sea Salt (Hawaiian)		Extracted from tidal pools that are lined with a small amount of red volcanic clay (which gives the salt its color) Commercial supplies come from Kauai and California
Fleur de Sel (French)		Hand harvested sea salt that is collected off the coast of Brittany, France The same method is used to harvest sea salt in Spain, Greece, and Canada
Celtic Sea Salt		Hand harvested sea salt that is collected off the coast of France The clay found in the salt flats responsible for the light grey color
Hiwa Kai Hawaiian Black Lava Salt		A blend of Hawaiian sea salt and purified Hawaiian volcanic charcoal Used as a "finishing salt" (sprinkled on raw, after cooking) for sushi, grilled steak, and veggies
Hawaiian Bamboo Jade Sea Salt		A blend of Hawaiian sea salt and bamboo leaf extract Used in Asian-inspired stir-frys, soups, and vegetable dishes Used in traditional Hawaiian dishes
Persian Blue Sea Salt		Comes from the Semman province of Northern Iran Contains a compound similar to crystallized potassium chloride (gives the salt its blue color)

What Makes Unrefined Sea Salt Special?

All of the above varieties fall under the umbrella term of "unrefined" sea salt. There are several uses and health benefits of sea salt that are still being investigated and are still under scrutiny. That being said, there are certain properties and benefits of sea salt that have already been established. The iodine in both natural sea salt and ordinary table salt helps promote optimal thyroid function.

However, during the refining process, minerals like magnesium, calcium, zinc, iron, potassium, and iodine are removed from table salt. This is why ordinary table salt is "iodized"; the manufacturers add the iodine back into the salt. This is similar to the way in which "enriched" or "fortified" products are made. Natural, unrefined sea salt retains these minerals. This promotes proper hydration, electrolyte balance, blood sugar regulation, and blood pressure regulation.

Guide to Grains Chart

GRAIN	WHAT IT LOOKS LIKE	GLUTEN FREE?	BENEFITS/DESCRIPTION	FORMS	HOW TO COOK IT
Wheat		NO	Whole grain and refined varieties. Can be a good source of vitamins, minerals, fiber, and complex carbohydrates	Flour, Cereals, Breads, Pasta	Traditional wheat cannot be used for cooking unless it is milled into a flour. See the "flours" chart for references and ideas. See the list of suggested recipes below. See the "wheat berres" section of this chart
Buckwheat		YES	Buckwheat is the seed of a flowering plant that is related to rhubarb and sorrel. Low glycemic index. High in protein. Gluten free	Flour, Flakes, Groats	**Groats Yield:** 1/2 C dry = 1 C cooked. **Groats Directions:** Add 1 C water to 1/2 C groats and simmer, covered, for 15 minutes. **Flakes Yield:** 1/2 C dry = 1 C cooked. **Flakes Directions:** Add 1 C water to 1/2 C flakes and bring to a boil. Reduce heat to low and simmer for 1-2 minutes, stirring occasionally
Rye		NO	Rye is a cereal grain that looks similar to wheat. Rich in vitamins, minerals, and fiber. Low glycemic index. Contains gluten	Flour, Bread, Flakes, Cracked, Kernels or Berries, Whisky	**Berries/Kernels Yield:** 1/2 C dry = 1 1/2 C cooked. **Berries Directions:** Add 1 1/2 C water to 1/2 C berries and simmer, covered, for 2 hours. **Flakes Yield:** 1 C dry = 4 C cooked. **Flakes Directions:** Bring 3 C water to a boil and add 1 C flakes. Reduce heat to low, cover and simmer for 15 minutes, stirring occasionally
Oats		YES	Oats are a cereal grain. Rich in fiber. Shown to help lower cholesterol. Good source of iron. Low glycemic index	Flour, Steel Cut (i.e. Irish or Scottish), Rolled	**Steel Cut Yield:** 1 C dry = 3 1/2 to 4 C cooked. **Steel Cut Directions:** Bring 3 1/2 to 4 C of water to a boil and add 1 C of steel cut oats. As the oats begin to thicken, reduce heat to low, cover, and simmer for 20-30 minutes. **Rolled Yield:** 2 C dry = 4 C cooked. **Rolled Directions:** Bring 3 1/4 C of water to a boil and add 2 C rolled oats. Reduce heat and simmer, uncovered for 5 minutes, stirring occasionally
Quinoa		YES	Quinoa is a grain grown for its edible seeds. Contains all 9 essential amino acids (a complete protein). White, red, and black varieties. Anti-inflammatory. Gluten Free	Flour, Red, Black, White	**Yield:** 1 C dry = 3 C cooked. **Directions:** Add 2 C water to 1 C dry Quinoa and bring to a boil. Cover and reduce heat to low. Simmer for about 15-2o minutes, then drain to remove excess water.
Teff		YES	The smallest grain in the world (about poppy-seed size). Grown (almost entirely) in Ethiopia and Eritrea. Good source of Calcium. White, red, and brown varieties. Gluten Free	Flour, Seed	**Seed Yield:** 1 C dry = 3 C cooked. **Seed Directions:** Toast 1 C teff in a frying pan over medium-low heat, for about 2 minutes, until it "pops". Transfer the teff to pot and add 3 C water. Bring to a boil, then reduce the heat to low, cover and simmer for 15-20 minutes until the water is absorbed. Remove from heat and let sit, covered, for 5 minutes.
Amaranth		YES	Amaranth is a grain native to Peru and South America. Originally grown by the Aztecs. High in protein and minerals. Low glycemic index. Shown to help lower blood pressure. Gluten Free	Flour, Seeds, Greens (similar to spinach or swiss chard)	**Seed Yield:** 1/2 C dry = 1 1/2 C cooked. **Seed Directions:** Place 1/2 C amaranth and 1 1/2 C water in a saucepan and bring to a boil. Reduce heat and simmer, uncovered for about 20 minutes, until the water is absorbed. **Greens Directions:** Heat oil in a skillet over medium-high heat. Add washed, chopped, or whole amaranth greens (de-stemmed), and saute until water has been released

Grain		Whole Grain	Description	Products	Directions
Barley		NO	Barley is a cereal grain used to make malted barley syrup Low glycemic index Shown to increase the amount of benefical gut bacteria	Flour Flakes Grits Pearl Hulled Whisky Beer	**Pearl Barley Yield:** 1/2 dry = 2 C cooked **Pear Barley Directions:** Add 1 1/2 C water to 1/2 C dry and simmer, uncovered, for 30-45 minutes. **Hulled Barley Yield:** 1/2 C dry = 1 1/4 C cooked **Hulled Barley Directions:** Add 2 C water to 1/2 C dry and simmer, covered, for 1 hour, 40 minutes
Millet		YES	Millet is a seed-like grain and is often sprinkled on top of bread before baking Low glycemic index Shown to improve heart health	Flour Seeds Flakes	**Seeds Yield:** 1 C dry = 3 C cooked **Seeds Directions:** Toast on medium heat for 4-6 minutes. Add 1 1/2 C to 2 1/2 C of water and simmer, uncovered for 13-18 minutes. Remove from heat and let stand for 10 minutes **Flakes Yield:** 1/2 C dry = 1 C cooked **Flakes Directions:** Bring 1/2 C flakes and 1 C water to a boil. Reduce heat and simmer for 8-10 minutes, stirring occasionally
Sorghum		YES	A grain group originally grown in Africa Rich in vitamins and minerals Good source of fiber Shown to improve circulation and bone health	Flour Seeds Flakes Syrup	**Seeds Yield:** 1 C dry = 2 1/2 C cooked **Boiling Directions:** Gently rinse and drain the sorghum. Add 3 C water to 1 C sorghum and bring to a boil. Cover, reduce the heat to low, and simmer for about 50 minutes to 1 hour. When the seeds have softened, drain any excess water. **Popping Directions:** Place a stainless steel pot over medium-high heat. Add the sorghum seeds and cover with a lid. Cook, shaking the pot often, until the sorghum seeds have popped. Remove from heat.
Triticale		NO	A hybrid grain made from a cross between rye and wheat First produced in the late 19th century in Scotland and Sweden Good source of protein Rich in vitamins and minerals	Flour Berries	**Berries Yield:** 1/2 C dry = 1 1/4 C cooked **Berries Directions:** Add 1 1/2 C water to 1/2 C triticale berries and simmer, covered, for 1 hour and 10 minutes, or until the water is absorbed.
White Rice		YES	Made by a milling process that removes the bran and germ Lower in phytic acid and easier to digest than brown rice High glycemic index	Flour Rice Paper Grain	**Grain Yield:** 1 C dry = 3 C cooked **Grain Directions:** Add 2 C water to 1 C rice and simmer for about 30 minutes on medium-low heat until the water is absorbed. Fluff with a fork before serving. **Rice Paper Directions:** Fill a shallow bowl or a skillet with very warm water (but not boiling) and slide a sheet of rice paper into the water. Submerge for 15-30 seconds, then carefully remove, gently tap off the excess water, and place on work surface.
Whole Grain Rice		YES	Brown, black, and red varieties Retains the bran and germ High in vitamins and minerals Good source of Fiber Good source of anitoxidants	Flour Rice Paper Grain	**Grain Yield:** 1 C dry = 3 C cooked **Grain Directions:** Add 2 1/4 C water to 1 C rice and simmer for 45 minutes on medium-low heat, until the water is absorbed. Fluff with a fork before serving.
Corn		YES	A grain crop originating from Mexico that is also called maize Yellow, white, blue, and red varieties Popcorn and sweetcorn varieties Good source of antioxidants Good source of fiber	Flour/meal Polenta Cob Masa harina Husk Hominy Grits	**Cob Directions (Boiled):** Husk the corn and remove threads. Place the cob(s) in a large pot, cover with water, and add a pinch of salt. Bring to a boil, cover, and reduce heat to medium low, simmering for about 5 minutes. Use tongs to remove. **Grits Yield:** 1 C dry = about 1 1/3 C cooked **Grits Directions:** Bring 4 1/2 C water to a boil. Reduce the heat to medium and slowly whisk in 1 C dry grits, stirring continuously for 3-5 minutes. Reduce the heat to low, and cook for 45-50 minutes, stirring continuously. Stir in seasonings/butter/milk, etc.

Name		Whole Grain	Description	Form	Directions
Wild Rice		YES	An aquatic grass related to traditional rice / High in protein / Richer in vitamins and minerals than traditional rice / Good source of fiber	Grain	**Grain Yield:** 1 C dry = 3 C cooked **Grain Directions:** Combine 1 C dry wild rice with 3 C water in a pot. Bring to a boil, then reduce heat, cover and simmer for 30-50 minutes, until the water is absorbed. Fluff with a fork before serving.
Bulgur		NO	A whole wheat grain that has been cracked and partially pre-cooked / Good source of fiber / Good source of Vitamin B-6 / Good source of iron	Fine Coarse Half-Cuts Kernel	**Kernel Yield:** 1 C dry = 2 C cooked **Directions:** Add 2 C water to 1 C bulgur and bring to a boil. Reduce heat to low, cover and let stand for 7 minutes.
Semolina		NO	Endosperm particles that are left over by milling durum wheat / Used to make pasta, cereal, couscous, and cream of wheat / Often sprinkled on pizza dough / Low glycemic index	Flour Kernels	There is no "basic" way to cook something like semolina kernels. See the "flours" chart for references See the recipes below for ideas on how to use semolina kernels
Kamut		NO	Also called Khorasan wheat or Pharoah grain / High in protein / High in beneficial fatty acids / Rich in vitamins and minerals / Low-Medium glycemic index	Flour Berries Flakes	**Berries Yield:** 1 C dry = 2 1/2 C cooked **Berries Directions:** Add 3 C water to 1 C berries. Bring to a boil. Cover and simmer on low for 1 1/2 to 2 hours, or until soft. Remove from heat, let stand for 15 minutes, and drain. **Flakes Yield:** 1 C dry = 2 1/2 C cooked **Flakes Directions:** Add 2 1/2 to 3 C water to 1 C flakes. Bring to a boil. Cover and simmer on low heat for 10-20 minutes. Remove from heat, let stand for a few minutes, and drain.
Farro		NO	A type of hulled wheat / Also called emmer / Good source of fiber / Good source of antioxidants / Good source of vitamins and minerals	Kernels	**Yield:** 2 C dry = 2 C cooked **Directions:** Add 2 1/2 C water to 1 C farro and simmer for 25-40 minutes on medium or medium-low heat
Wheat Berries		NO	A whole wheat kernel that contains the bran, germ, and endosperm (but no the hull) / Good source of fiber / Good source of protein / Good source of vitamins	Kernels	**Yield:** 1 C dry = 2 C cooked **Directions:** Add 2 1/2 C water to 1 C wheat berries and simmer for 45-60 minutes on medium low/low heat
Durum Wheat		NO	A variety of hard wheat grown in arid climates / Used to make pasta and bread / Milled to make semolina / Higher in protein that traditional wheat	Flour Kernels	Durum wheat cannot be used unless it has been milled into a flour. See the "flours" chart for references See the list of recipes below for ideas on how to use durum wheat

Grain Based Flours Chart

FLOUR	DESCRIPTION	BEST USES
All-Purpose Flour	Neutral flavor and soft texture Does not contain the germ or bran "Enriched" with vitamins and minerals that are lost during the refining process "Bleached" or "Unbleached" varieties Contains gluten	Breads, cookies, muffins, quick breads, pie crusts, thickening for sauces
Cake Flour or Pastry Flour	Neutral flavor and fine texture High starch content Contains gluten	Keeps cakes and pastries soft and helps them hold their shape
Bread Flour	Slightly sweet flavor Unbleached, high-gluten blend of 99.8% hard wheat flour Contains malted barley flour	Baking bread- the high gluten content and Potassium Bromate helps increase the elasticity of the dough
Self-Rising Flour	Neutral flavor All-purpose flour with added salt and baking powder Contains gluten	Baking quick breads and yeast breads
All-Purpose 100% Whole Wheat Flour	Usually stone-ground Coarse texture and nutty flavor Higher in vitamins, minerals, and fiber than white, All-purpose flour	Breads, cookies, muffins, quick breads, pie crusts
Buckwheat Flour	Fine texture Rich, earthy, nutty flavor Good source of fiber and protein Gluten Free	Pancakes, waffles, crepes, muffins, breads, cookies, cakes
Dark Rye Flour	Rich, hearty flavor Good source of copper and zinc Gluten Free	Bread, stollen, cakes, pancakes, waffles, cookies, muffins, crusts

Grain Based Flours Chart (Continued)

FLOUR	DESCRIPTION	BEST USES
Quinoa Flour	Earthy, nutty flavor Delicate texture Contains all 9 essential amino acids Gluten Free	Quick breads, cookies, muffins, pancakes, crusts, tortillas, cakes
Amaranth Flour	Nutty, malt-like flavor Contains all 9 essential amino acids Good source of iron and magnesium Gluten Free	Combine with another gluten-free flour or starch for baking Cakes, cookies, muffins, pancakes, crusts, tortillas
Millet Flour	Mild flavor Good source of protein Good source of phosphorous Gluten Free	Cakes, cookies, muffins, breads, scones
White Rice Flour	Light, mild flavor Smooth texture Easy to digest Gluten Free	Muffins, cookies, pastries, cakes, crusts, breads, scones, biscuits
Brown Rice Flour	Mild, nutty flavor Good source of protein Good source of iron	Muffins, cookies, pastries, cakes, crusts, breads, scones, biscuits
Semolina Flour	Buttery flavor Fine texture High in gluten	Bread and pasta (the high gluten content creates a very elastic dough that resists breaking)
Durum Wheat Flour	Fine texture and distinct flavor Good source of protein Contains gluten	Bread, pasta, pizza crust

Grain Based Flours Chart (Continued)

FLOUR	DESCRIPTION	BEST USES
Corn Flour	Finely textured version of stone-ground cornmeal Good source of fiber Sweet flavor and dense texture Gluten Free	Corn bread Breading meats in combination with other flour Waffles, muffins, cakes, biscuits, scones
Spelt Flour	Nutty flavor, coarse texture Good source of manganese and fiber Contains gluten	Breads, muffins, cookies, waffles, pasta, crusts
Sorghum Flour	Similar flavor to cornmeal Good source of protein Good source of iron Gluten Free	Injera breads, cookies, cakes, muffins, quick breads, biscuits
Sprouted Wheat Flour	Sweet, nutty flavor Soft texture Good source of vitamins and minerals Contains gluten	Breads, muffins, quick breads
Barley Flour	Sweet, nutty flavor Soft texture Good source of fiber Contains gluten	Substitute 1/3 C barley flour in place of All-Purpose flour when making biscuits, pancakes, muffins, cookies, and breads
Oat Flour	Sweet, mild flavor Good source of protein Good source of fiber Gluten Free	Breads, muffins, cookies, cakes pie crusts, pancakes, scones
Teff Flour	Fine texture Sweet, malty flavor Good source of protein and calcium Gluten Free	Injera bread, cakes, cookies, crusts brownies

Grain-Free Flours Chart

FLOUR	DESCRIPTION	BEST USES
Coconut Flour	Produced by grinding dried, de-fatted, coconut meat light, sweet flavor Good source of fiber Low in carbohydrates Gluten Free	Cakes, cookies, crusts, muffins breads, scones Goes well with tropical flavors, dark chocolate, and coffee
Almond Flour	Produced by grinding whole, blanched almonds Traditionally used to make French macarons Good source of Vitamin E Low in carbohydrates Gluten Free	Cakes, cookies, crusts, muffins breads, scones Use in place of breadcrumbs to coat meats and fish
Hazelnut Flour	Produced by grinding whole hazelnuts Rich, buttery flavor Good source of Vitamin E Low in carbohydrates Gluten Free	Cakes, cookies, crusts, muffins breads, scones dukkah spice mix
Pecan Flour	Produced by grinding whole whole pecans Rich, nutty flavor Good source of fiber Good source of Phosphorus Low in carbohydrates Gluten Free	Cakes, cookies, crusts, muffins breads, scones As a topping for fruit crisps and crumbles
Walnut Flour	Produced by grinding whole walnuts Rich, earthy flavor Good source of Omega 3's Low in carbohydrates Gluten Free	Cakes, cookies, crusts, muffins breads, scones Goes well with caramel, chocolate, and blackberries

Grain-Free Flours Chart (Continued)

FLOUR	DESCRIPTION	BEST USES
Flaxseed Meal	Produced by grinding whole, cold-milled flaxseed Mild, nutty flavor Good source of Omega 3's Good source of Fiber Gluten Free	Cakes, cookies, muffins, crusts, breads Add a spoonful to your smoothie Use 1T flaxseed meal and 3T water as an egg replacement for baking
Chestnut Flour	Made from whole, peeled, dehydrated chestnuts Commonly used in italian baked goods Sweet, creamy flavor Good source of Manganese Gluten Free	Cakes, cookies, muffins, breads, scones
Potato or Sweet Potato Flour	Made from ground, whole, peeled potatoes (typically russet potatoes) Good source of B Vitamins Mild flavor Often used in gluten free baking to increase moisture content Gluten Free	Breads, pancakes, muffins, soups, biscuits
Pistachio Flour	Made from ground pistachios Often combined with almond flour to make pistachio flavored French macarons Good source of Vitamin B-6 Nutty, toasty flavor Gluten Free	Cakes, cookies, muffins
Chickpea Flour	Made from dried, stone ground, garbanzo beans (chickpeas) Good source of fiber Good source of iron Good source of protein Gluten Free	Crusts, falafel papadums, pakoras, cookies, breads

De-Coding Milk Chart

MILK	DESCRIPTION	PROS	CONS	LACTOSE FREE?
Cow's Milk	Whole, 2%, and skim varieties Raw and pasteurized varieties Used to make cheese, yogurt, and butter	Good source of Calcium Good source of Vitamin B12 Good source of Phosphorus Good source of protein	Acidic properties that may be harmful May contain artificial hormones, steroids, or antibiotics (depending on the brand/source)	NO
Goat's Milk	Raw and pasteurized varities Used to make cheese, yogurt, and butter	Good source of Calcium Good souce of protein Good souce of Phosphorus Good source of Riboflavin About 10% less lactose than Cow's milk	Decreases Vitamin B12 absorption Higher in fat than Cow's milk Not suitable for infants	NO
Sheep's Milk	Raw and pasteurized varieties Used to make cheese, yogurt, and butter	Contains nearly twice as many minerals as Cow's milk including: Calcium, Phosphorous, and Zinc Good source of Iodine Good source of Vitamin B12 Good source of protein	Contains nearly twice as much fat as Cow's milk Not suitable for infants About the same amount of lactose as Cow's milk	NO
Almond Milk	Made by blending whole, soaked almonds with water	Good source of Calcium Good source of Vitamin E Low in Calories	Not a good source of protein Store bought brands often contain lots of additives	YES
Hazelnut Milk	Made by blending whole, soaked hazelnuts with water	Good source of Calcium Good source of Magnesium Low in fat	Not a good source of protein Store bought brands often contain lots of additives	YES
Cashew Milk	Made by blending whole, soaked cashews with water	Good source of Calcium Good source of Selenium Low in fat	Not a good source of protein Store bought brands often contain lots of additives	YES

De-Coding Milk Chart (Continued)

MILK	DESCRIPTION	PROS	CONS	LACTOSE FREE?
Rice Milk	Made by blending and straining boiled rice and water	Cholesterol Free	Not a good source of protein Not a significant amount of any vitamins or minerals but is sometimes fortified Store bought brands often contain lots of additives	YES
Oat Milk	Made by blending and straining oats and water	Good Source of Folate (Vitamin B9) Cholesterol Free	Not a good source of protein Not a good source of Calcium (unless fortified)	YES
Hemp Milk	Made by blending and straining hemp seeds and water	Good source of Iron Good source of Omega 3's Good source of protein	Not a good source of Calcium (unless fortified)	YES
Coconut Milk	Made by straining the liquid from inside a whole coconut to separate the milk, cream, and water	Good source of Iron	Not a good source of protein High in saturated fat	YES
Soy Milk	Made by blending and soaking soy beans and water	Good source of Calcium	Contains isoflavones which may increase the risk of estrogen-based cancers	YES

Your Guide to Homemade Non-Dairy Milk

BASE	SOAKING TIME	WATER NEEDED FOR BLENDING	METHOD
Almonds	8-12 hours	4 C water per 2 C nuts	1. Soak base for the appropriate time
Cashews	2 hours	4 C water per 2 C nuts	2. Drain through a colander and rinse
Hazelnuts	8 hours	4 C water per 2 C nuts	3. Put the base, water, and any
Pistachios	None	3 C water per 2 C nuts	desired flavorings into a blender
Walnuts	4 hours	4 C water per 2 C nuts	4. Cover and blend on high for 2-3 min.
Hemp Seeds	None	2 C water per 1/4 C hemp seeds	5. Strain through a cheesecloth or
Oats	30 minutes	3 C water per 1 C oats	fine mesh strainer into a bowl.
Cooked Rice	None	4 C water per 1 C cooked rice	6. Refrigerate in sealed glass container.

The Glycemic Index

GLYCEMIC INDEX SCALE
LOW GI DEFINED AS <55
MEDIUM GI DEFINED AS 56-69
HIGH GI DEFINED AS 70-100

The glycemic index is a ranking system used to analyze foods that contain carbohydrates.
It measures the degree to which a food affects one's blood sugar levels.
Foods with a high glycemic index are digested rapidly and cause a large insulin spike,
while foods with a low glycemic index are digested slowly and cause a much smaller rise in insulin levels.

Foods that do not have a glycemic index are those that don't contain carbohydrates.
The point of this chart is not to say that certain foods are "bad", and certain foods are "good".
The point is to give you information so that you can make educated choices.
High glycemic index foods can play a very important role in
sports/athletic performance as can medium and low glycemic index foods.

The glycemic index scale ranges from 0 to 100
(where 0 would be something like chicken, and 100 would be something like pure glucose/sugar).
Keep in mind that the "high", "medium", and "low", ranks are estimates.
See the "Glycemic Load" chart on the following pages for more information.

HIGH GI EXAMPLES	MEDIUM GI EXAMPLES	LOW GI EXAMPLES	ZERO GI EXAMPLES
Russet Potatoes	Beets	Nuts and seeds	Beef
Parsnips	Orange juice	Broccoli	Bison
Cane sugar (all forms)	Bananas	Leafy greens	Pork
French Fries	Sweet potatoes	Apples	Fish
Rice cakes	Yams	Pears	Chicken
Pretzels	Pineapple	Oranges	Turkey
Cornflakes	Oats	Cherries	Lamb
Instant mashed potatoes	Whole Wheat Bread	Plain yogurt	Duck
White rice	Rye	Lentils	Eggs
Dates	Buckwheat	Dark chocolate	Cheeses
Watermelon	Brown rice		
Corn chips	Kiwifruit		
Candy	Raisins		
Any bread, pastry, cake, cookie, etc.	Honey		
made with refined white flour	Molasses		
and cane sugar	Coconut sugar		
	Brown rice syrup		

The Glycemic Load

GLYCEMIC LOAD SCALE
LOW: 10 OR LESS
MEDIUM: 11 TO 19
HIGH: 20 OR MORE

The glycemic load is a more practical and application version of the glycemic index. It is measured by multiplying a food's glycemic index (as a percentage) by the "total net carbs" of the food. This is because fiber helps slow down digestion and absorption of nutrients. Hence, something that has a high glycemic index may have a medium glycemic load.

Another thing to note is, since the equation uses "net grams of carbohydrate", this means that the glycemic load takes portion size into consideration. As such, a smaller amount of a high glycemic food, will have a smaller glycemic load. As the portion size decreases, so does the glycemic load. The chart below uses white rice (a high glycemic index food) to show how serving size influences glycemic load.

Estimated Glycemic Load Calculator
You can use this equation to estimate the glycemic load of a specific food:

$$\frac{Glycemic\ Index\ Value \times Net\ Grams\ of\ Carbohydrate}{100} = Glycemic\ Load$$

$$Net\ Grams\ of\ Carbohydrate = Total\ Grams\ of\ Carbohydrate - Total\ Grams\ of\ Fiber$$

EXAMPLE FOOD: WHITE RICE	
SERVING SIZE	GLYCEMIC LOAD
1/2 C	35
2/3 C	56
1 C	70

Extra Tips to Decrease Glycemic Load:
- *Eating high glycemic foods with low glycemic foods helps slow down digestion and reduce blood sugar spikes.*
  ***Examples:** Top white bread (high glycemic index food) with mashed avocado (low glycemic index food), or add grilled vegetables (low glycemic index food) to white rice (high glycemic index food).*

- *Sprinkling cinnamon on top of high or medium glycemic index foods helps to keep blood sugar levels stable.*
- *See the "Spices" chart on pg.160 for more information.*

Glycemic Index of Sweeteners

SWEETENER	GI
Granulated Sugar	64
Powdered Sugar	64
Brown Sugar	64
Raw Sugar	64
Evaporated Cane Juice	55
Agave Nectar	15
Honey	30

SWEETENER	GI
Maple Syrup	54
Blackstrap Molasses	55
Brown Rice Syrup	25
Malted Barley Syrup	42
Stevia	Less than 1
Coconut Sugar	35
Jerusalem Artichoke Syrup	Less than 10

INDEX

INGREDIENT SOURCING
Some Of My Favorite Brands and Resources
These brands are offered online, or at certain retailers listed on their websites.

- **Kerrygold**
 http://www.kerrygoldusa.com
 Offers grass fed butter and cheese from Ireland

- **Bob's Red Mill**
 http://www.bobsredmill.com/
 Offers nut flours and nut meals, oats, cereals, mixes, grain-based flours, gluten free products, beans, seeds, etc.

- **Authentic Foods**
 http://www.authenticfoods.com/
 Offers nut flours, bean flours, grain-based flours, baking mixes, gluten free products, etc.

- **Arrowhead Mills**
 http://www.arrowheadmills.com/
 Offers nut flours, grain-based flours, gluten free products, nut butters, baking mixes, etc.

- **Omega Nutrition**
 http://www.omeganutrition.com/
 Offers seed butters, cooking oils, vinegars, sea salts, culture starters, etc.

- **Cultures of Health**
 http://www.culturesforhealth.com/
 Offers culture starts for sourdough, cheese, kefir, yogurt, buttermilk, fermented vegetables, kefir, kombucha, etc.
 Offers instructions for making your own cultures at home

- **Local Harvest**
  http://www.localharvest.org/farmers-markets/
  Helps you find your nearest farmers' market

- **Harmless Harvest**
  http://www.harmlessharvest.com/
  Though it is on the expensive side, this is a great brand of coconut water that is 100% raw and unprocessed

- **Jubali**
  http://www.jubali.org/
  Offers additive free

and smoothies
   Part of a café based out of Boston, MA
   Available for online order

- **Organic Valley**
  https://www.organicvalley.coop/products/
  Offers organic, grass fed milk and dairy products

- **Eat Wild**
  http://www.eatwild.com/index.html
  Helps you find grass fed meats, eggs, and dairy products in your Area

- **Honey**
  http://www.honey.com/honey-locator/
  Helps you find local honey suppliers in your area

- **Kitchen Dial**
  An app that helps you convert between grams, ounces, pounds, liters, cups, pints, quarts, and gallons

Good Quality Brands of Puff Pastry/Frozen Dough

These brands are free from things like additives, artificial ingredients, trans fat, bleached flour, and high fructose corn syrup. Many of these brands are offered online via Amazon, or at certain retailers specified by their websites.

- **Wewalka:** http://wewalka.us/
  Offers refrigerated puff pastry, pizza dough, and croissant dough

- **Dufour:**
  http://www.dufourpastrykitchens.com/index.html
  Offers Kosher products
  Offers puff pastry and several types of tart shells

- **Carême:** http://caremepastry.com/classic-pastry-products/all-butter-puff-pastry/
  Offers gluten free puff pastry

- **The Filo Factory:** http://www.fillofactory.com/
  Offers puff pastry, filo dough, and frozen appetizers

- **Gee Free Foods:** http://geefreefoods.com/
  Makes gluten free products

- **Aussie Bakery:** http://www.aussiebakery.com/
  Offers vegan products

TRADITIONAL PUFF PASTRY
Makes About 1 lb.

INGREDIENTS
- 1 C unbleached all-purpose flour
- 2/3 C ice cold water
- 8 T cold, unsalted butter
- pinch of sea salt

DIRECTIONS
Sift the flour and salt together in a medium bowl. Cut the butter into cubes, and add it to the flour and salt mixture. Using your hand like a whisk, gently turn the butter into the flour and salt mixture, until the butter is broken down into small, pea-sized pieces. The dough will be very crumbly at this stage.

Make a well in the center, and pour in the water. Use a fork and stir until incorporated. Place the dough onto a floured cutting board. Pat it into a rough, square shape.

Using a floured rolling pin, roll the dough out into a rectangle that is about 10 inches long. Take the bottom third of the dough, and fold it over the middle. Do the same with the top third of the dough.

Rotate the dough 90 degrees, and fold again, using the same method. Roll the dough out with a rolling pin, and repeat the folding technique 5 more times.

Wrap the dough with plastic wrap, and refrigerate for at least one hour, or overnight. You can also put the dough in the freezer at this point, where it will keep for about 1 month.

When you're ready to use the dough, remove it from the fridge and allow it to come to room temperature. Roll out onto a floured surface and use as desired.

GLUTEN FREE PUFF PASTRY
Makes About 1 ½ lb.

INGREDIENTS
- 30 T Gluten-Free Flour Blend (this is 2 C minus 2 T)
- pinch of sea salt
- 1 C cold, unsalted butter (16T)
- ½ C ice cold water

DIRECTIONS
Follow the directions for the "Traditional Puff Pastry" on pg. 183.

For The Gluten Free Flour Blend
- *1 ½ C brown rice flour*
- *½ C white rice flour*
- *½ C potato starch*
- *1 t baking powder*

Sift all of the ingredients together in a large bowl until well combined. For storage, transfer to an airtight container.

Note: *You can also buy pre-made gluten-free flour blends. A great brand is "Cup 4 Cup". You can substitute it for traditional flour in a 1:1 ratio.* http://www.cup4cup.com/

VEGAN PUFF PASTRY
Makes About 1 lb.

INGREDIENTS
- 2 C unbleached, all-purpose flour
- pinch of sea salt
- ¾ C solid coconut oil
- ¼ C ice cold water

DIRECTIONS
Follow the directions for the "Traditional Puff Pastry" on pg. 183.

REFERENCES

"A Guide to the B Vitamins". *Naturemade.com.* Pharmavite. n.d. Web. 8 June 2016.

"Amaranth". Photograph. *Mercola.* n.d. Web. 28 June 2016.

"Blue Salt". Photograph. *Stockmediators.com.* n.d. Web. 28 June 2016.

"Brown Rice". Photograph. *Care2* 6 July 2011. Web. 26 June 2016.

Brussell, Laura. "Teff". Photograph. April 2015. Web. 28 June 2016.

Bruso, Jessica. "How to Boost Zinc Absorption". *SF Gate.* n.d. Web. 21 June 2016.

"Buckwheat". Photograph. *Huffingtonpost.* 8 July 2015. Web. 28 June 2016.

Campbell, Meg. "Does Vitamin C Increase Iron Absorption?".*SF Gate* n.d. Web. 20 June 2016.

 "Cayenne Pepper". Photograph. *Coopercomplete* n.d. Web. 28 June 2016.

"Celtic Sea Salt". Photograph. *goodonyaorganic.com.* n.d. Web. 28 June 2016.

Chase , Brad. "Eating These Foods May Help You Sleep". *Progressive Health.* n.d. Web. 15 May 2016.

"Chronic Fatigue Syndrome: Who's at Risk?".*cdc.gov.* Centers for Disease Control and

        Prevention. 14 February 2013. Web. 24 June 2016.

"Cilantro". Photograph. *gertens.com.* n.d. Web. 29 June 2016.

"Cloves-Whole Ground". Photograph. *blogs.bu.edu* May 2011. Web. 28 June 2016.

Connor, Steve. "Anxiety and Depression Caused by Stress Linked to Gut Bacteria Living in Intestines,

        Scientists Find". *Independent* 28 July 2015. Web. 29 June 2016.

Conrad-Stoller, Jessica. "Microbes Help Produce Serotonin in the Gut". *Caltech. edu.* 9 April 2015. Web.

        29 June 2016.

"Corn Kernels". Photograph. *motherearthnews* n.d. Web. 25 June 2016.

"Dill Weed". Photograph. *images.wisegeek.com.* n.d. Web. 28 June 2016.

"Diphenhydramine". *WebMD.* WebMD, n.d. Web. 25 April 2016.

Doyle, Marek. "Help Me Sleep: Magnesium Is the Secret for Sleep Problems". *Huffpost Lifestyle* 22 July

    2013: Web.

"Durum Wheat". Photograph. *Buhlergroup.* n.d. Web. 24 June 2016.

"Fatigue Statistics". *tac.vic.gov.* Transit Accident Commission. n.d. Web 23 June 2016.

Felicetti, Marcus Julian. "6 Powerful Ways to Boost Your Magnesium Levels". *Mindbodygreen.com.* 22

    July 2012. Web. 28 April 2016.

George Mateljan. *Whfoods.com.* The George Mateljan Foundation. Web. 8 May 2016.

"Grains-Millet". *Shutterstock* 4 March 2015. Web. 28 June 2016.

Group, Edward. "15 Foods High in Vitamin E". *globalhealingcenter.com.* n.d. Web. 10 May 2016.

Hadhazy, Adam. "Think Twice: How the Gut's 'Second Brain' Influences Mood and Well-Being".

    Scientific American 12 February 2010. Web. 24 June 2016.

Haiken, Melanie. "5 Foods that Help You Sleep". *Caring.com.* Caring Inc. n.d. Web. 1 May 2016.

"Himalayan Pink Salt". Photograph. *frontiercoop.com.* n.d. Web. 28 June 2016.

Hitti, Miranda. "Grapes May Help With Sleep". *Cbsnews.com.* WebMD. 19 June 2006. Web. 2 June

    2016.

House, Paul, and Whitbread, Daisy. *Healthaliciousness.com.* USDA National Nutrient Database.

    n.d.Web. 5 May 2016.

Juurikas, Imeline. "Ginger" Photograph. *Looduspere.* 2015. Web. 28 June 2016.

"Kamut Grain Close Up". Photograph. *Wisegeek* n.d. Web. 25 June 2016.

"Lavender Flower". Photograph. *everything-lavender.com.* n.d. Web. 28 June 2016.

"Lunesta Side Effects". *Drugs.com.* Drugs.com. Web. 24 April 2016.

"Marjoram". Photograph. *essentialoilspedia.com.* n.d. Web. 29 June 2016.

Maskell, James. "Top 10 Probiotic Foods to Add to Your Diet". *Mindbodygreen.com.* 2 May 2013. Web. 29 June 2016.

"Milk, whole, 3.25% milkfat Nutrition Facts and Calories". *Self.com.* Self Nutrition Data. n.d. Web. 26 April 2016.

Morris, York Susan. "Vitamins for Energy: Does B12 Work?" *healthline.com.* 7 August 2014. Web. 21 June 2016.

"Oregano Leaves". Photograph. *Medicalnewstoday.com.* n.d. Web. 28 June 2016.

"Paprika Powder". Photograph. *actvebeat.com.* August 2015. Web. 28 June 2016.

"Parsley". Photograph. *gourmetgarden.com.* n.d. Web. 28 June 2016.

"Pile of Sorghum Grain". *Wisegeek* n.d. Web. 29 June 2016.

"Products". Photograph. *cdn2bigcommerce.com.* n.d. Web. 28 June 2016.

"Red Aleala Salt Product". Photograph. *mountainroseherbs.com.* n.d. Web. 28 June 2016.

Romm, Cari. "Americans Are Getting Worse At Taking Sleeping Pills". *The Atlantic* 12 August 2014: Web.

"Rosemary 2". Photograph. *organicfacts.net.* n.d. Web. 28 June 2016.

"Rozerem Side Effects". *Drugs.com.* Drugs.com. n.d. Web. 24 April 2016.

"Rye Kernels'. Photograph. *Cdn* n.d. Web. 28 June 2016.

"Sea Salt Hawaiian Black Lava". Photograph. *savoryspiceshop.com.* n.d. Web. 28 June 2016.

"Sleeping Pills: What You Need to Know". *WebMD.*WebMD. n.d.25 April 2016.

"Tarragon". Photograph. *fruitandvegetablesmelbourne.com.au.* January 2015. Web. 28 June 2016.

"The Four Corners Peppercorn Blend". Photograph. *Savoryspiceshop.* 3 May 2015. Web. 28 June 2016.

"Thyme 3". Photograph. *gourmetgarden.com.* n.d. Web. 28 June 2016.

"Uploads". Photograph. *formaggiokitchen.com.* February 2011. Web. 28 June 2016.

"Vanilla Bean and Orchid". Photograph. *Hawaiianvanilla.com.* n.d. Web. 28 June 2016.

"Vegetarian". Photograph. *f.tqn.* n.d. Web. 28 June 2016.

"Vitamin B12". *nlm.nih.gov.* US National Library of Medicine. n.d. Web 22 June 2016.

"What is Quinoa". Photograph. *Dailyquinoa* May 2015. Web. 28 June 2016.

"Wheat". Photograph. *Shreekalalglobal,* 2013. Web. 28 June 2016.

"Wheat Berries Adjusted for Color and Resized". Photograph. n.d. Web. 24 June 2016.

"World Record Basil Leaf". Photograph. *bigbudsmag.com.* n.d. Web. 28 June 2016.

Printed in Great Britain
by Amazon